CW01455107

Time is in His Hands

Time is in His Hands

An Advent to Epiphany Devotional

KATE EVANS

THE CHOIR PRESS

Copyright © 2025 Kate Evans

All rights reserved. No part of this publication may be reproduced or transmitted in any form or by any means, electronic or mechanical including photocopying, recording or any information storage or retrieval system, without prior permission in writing from the publishers.

The right of Kate Evans to be identified as the author of this work has been asserted by her in accordance with the Copyright, Designs and Patents Act 1988

First published in the United Kingdom in 2025 by
The Choir Press

ISBN 978-1-78963-557-7

Unless otherwise stated, Scripture quotations are taken from the Holy Bible, New International Version® Anglicized, NIV®. Copyright © 1979, 1984, 2011 by Biblica, Inc.® Used by permission. All rights reserved worldwide.

Written for my daughters,
Rhiannon and Lydia,
who have been a source of great encouragement and
inspiration over years of writing and pondering,

and in gratitude to:

my parents,
John and Marilyn Skinner,
who introduced me to the Lord Jesus at a very young age,
mirrored his characteristics to me in their lives,
and taught me from his precious word;

my husband and soulmate,
David,
whose extraordinary patience, wisdom and staunch support
has been unwavering and without whose help this would
never have come to fruition;

all those who offered to read through my initial manuscript
and spurred me on to consider wider publication;

my editor,
Julie Hatherall,
whose expertise and wise advice have been invaluable.

Dedicated to

Erinna Pilbeam

who, despite the most unimaginable adversity,
continues to hold steadfastly to the Lord
and is an inspiration to my family and many others.

Contents

PREFACE

'Take time out'

When discussing past events within the family, my husband David and I sometimes need to clarify: 'Did that happen pre-accident or post-accident?'

In February 1999 we were hit head on by a drunk driver, who collided with our car on our side of the road. We had just set off on a Friday evening for supper with the parents of a pupil in the boys' boarding house David ran with my support. David was at the wheel, while I was clutching flowers and wine in my hands. The collision inflicted terrible injuries on us both and then plunged us, thankfully, into temporary oblivion.

In retrospect, we can see the many provisions which the Lord had set in place before that night occurred, as well as the many ways in which he intervened at the time. We feel reassured that God had prepared in advance for this life-changing event – almost giving us a brief glimpse, as it were, right into the heavenly planning centre and his detailed spreadsheet. (I have written much more about this in the Appendix for anyone who would like to know more.) We can also trace very clearly God's hand in all the events of that evening. That has often given us wonderful comfort.

The collision was to have massive repercussions, not only in our own lives but in those of our family and many in the community where we lived and worked. Yet although it was a terrible thing that happened to us, we believe that God was totally in control and that everything was filtered through his hands.

Now, as we begin the season of Advent, we can have the privilege of insight into the greatest heavenly spreadsheet of all time (or indeed outside time!). On a far, far greater and wonderful scale we see the pieces set in place for the most momentous, systemic shift in history: the turning point from 'pre' to 'post' the coming of Jesus, from what we know as BC to AD.

We can zoom out to see the big picture: history 'before Christ', occurring over hundreds of years before his coming down to earth and taking on human form. We can see scribes faithfully recording prophecies centuries before Jesus' birth, indicating how and where he would be born and details of his life that could not possibly have been known in advance. We can see the foreshadowing of Jesus in other people's lives. We can marvel at the events perfectly set in place, showing how God was totally in control of history. As Galatians 4:4 says, *'when the set time had fully come, God sent his Son'*. God had everything prepared for events to then unfold as BC silently shifted to AD.

Zooming in more closely, we can see political events and geographical details converging at a point in time. Augustus discusses with his advisors about the possibility of a census over his vast empire, after the Romans have taken over control of the Jewish homeland and exile has scattered people away from their homes. Trade routes enable widespread communication. Literacy has advanced to allow the accurate recording of events. Zechariah and Elizabeth get married and try for a family for many years, with no success. A group of men hundreds of miles away in Persia/Syria develop their interest in astrology, then act on what they believe is being shown to them. Betrothal discussions take place leading to Joseph and Mary's engagement. A faithful remnant of God's believing people, like Simeon and Anna, pray year after year that he would send the Messiah.

The political, geographical and historical scenes are set in place, and the Romans are in power with the most abhorrent means of execution ever devised. So please come and join with me in marvelling at God's sovereign plan, as we explore both the big picture and the tiny details in the divine spreadsheet. All the pieces culminate in the most incredible, panoramic picture of all time.

Dim the lights, raise the curtain and come with me to the hill country of Judea …

The following Bible readings begin on 1 December and continue through to Epiphany on 6 January. Each day has reflections, often containing questions to consider, to help us think how to apply that passage to our lives. Next is a suggested song to listen to as a reminder during the day. (These can easily be found online, but we've compiled a Spotify playlist that includes them all – just search for 'Time is in His Hands' on the Spotify app. or use the QR code below) The final element is a name of God or Jesus on which to meditate. I hope that you will find some or all of these helpful.

1 DECEMBER

'Perfect timing'

The intricate plan of the God who is outside time

Before the mountains were born
or you brought forth the whole world,
from everlasting to everlasting you are God ...
A thousand years in your sight
are like a day that has just gone by.

PSALM 90:2, 4

On this first day of December, I want to start by encouraging us to zoom out, perhaps as far as it is possible for us humanly to do, and to spend some time considering how big our view of God is. Advent encourages us to think about the plan of a sovereign God, who is high over all, unimaginably great, and eternal and everlasting – as the reading for today proclaims. And this God chose to reveal himself to us.

Devon and Cornwall have to be high up on my list of favourite places for their stunning coastal views and fabulous beaches. I love being by the sea, and hearing and watching the crash of the waves on the rocks. I am in awe of the certainty that the tide will draw in and out with the exact timings the moon dictates, and the sun will rise and set, often to a blaze of spectacular colour, to the minutes already predestined. These things have remained constant for thousands of years, regardless of events in the world, my life and the lives of those around me.

1

Nature gives perspective to my concerns and helps me to view them in the bigger picture. Periodic 'times out', regularly built into the diary in order to do this, are essential for me. They are time to reassess, time to ponder, time to process.

John Stott, the late church leader, used to start his morning time of prayer with the words 'Almighty God, Creator and Sustainer of the Universe, I worship you'. I have tried to adopt this myself because it sets the rest of the day in perspective. An ascending plane rises up through the cloud to stunningly bright sunshine, reminding us that the brilliance of the sun is a constant (however much the clouds may hide it from the earth). In the same way, it helps me to take time to rise above the busyness of each day.

The fact that ours is only one of a hundred billion galaxies in the universe God created reminds us of how tiny and insignificant we are on planet earth. Yet God has declared that he loves mankind so much that he wants to communicate with us. More than that, he stepped onto our earth for thirty or so years of history to live among us and to reveal his plan to us. Given this, it is of immeasurable importance for us to listen to what he has to say.

God knows that we need to dwell in his word. Presumably one of the reasons why you have prioritised the discipline of daily readings for Advent is because you realise the importance of gaining perspective on what matters in life. And what could be more important than to focus on what God declares through his son Jesus – his becoming one of us, living among us, dying for us, rising again and promising to return to judge the world and wrap up history?

This is the intention of the season of Advent: to take a few minutes each day to regain perspective, to ponder, to reflect, to wonder at and to prepare for the Lord Jesus' return.

And our God is a God of exact and perfect timings. Time

is so important: time to meditate, time to process, time to grapple with difficult concepts and challenging circumstances. Knowing this, God's plan of coming to earth was revealed very early on in history, a little at a time. This gave human beings time to reflect, to discuss, to repent and to respond as they listened to the words that God said through the prophets over the years.

So let's metaphorically keep two lenses open – one wide, one microscopic – as we commit to taking time out each day to focus on who God is and what he might be saying afresh to us this Advent season. Let's wonder again at his awesome and everlasting greatness, and at his exact and perfect timings.

Song: 'Everlasting God' by Chris Tomlin

Name to ponder: **'Everlasting God'** (Isaiah 40:28)

'Long time no hear'

400 years and counting ...

... the mystery that has been kept hidden for
ages and generations, but is now disclosed to
the Lord's people.

COLOSSIANS 1:26

We can all find waiting hard, can't we? Waiting is frustrating
and can bring with it an inclination to lose focus or hope.

When push came to shove for Edward VIII, love and
passion won his heart and mind over duty and allegiance. He
chose to marry the divorcee Wallis Simpson and so abdi-
cated, propelling his younger brother to the throne as George
VI. Once he died and Elizabeth II was on the throne, her son
Charles became heir apparent. Though just three, his carefree childhood days were over and his kingly training began.
King Charles III broke all existing records, waiting for a total
of seven decades (plus 274 days!) to ascend to the throne
himself at the grand age of seventy-three, when most of his
contemporaries were well into their retirement. The wait was
no doubt a long and sometimes even tortuous one for him.

The Jewish nation was used to waiting. We are not. Even
the pages of the first books of the Bible tell of waits for promised events to occur: Abram waiting twenty-five years for his
barren wife to conceive the baby God had promised them;[1]
and the Israelites in Egypt as slaves for 400 years before they

experienced the freedom that had been predicted for them.[2] But add another thousand years and we have the length of time God's people had been waiting for the arrival of a person called the 'Messiah'.

The Jewish nation had seen many predictions fulfilled over the years, but over and over again mention had been made of the arrival of a special messenger from God, sometimes called an 'Anointed One' (or 'Messiah' in Hebrew, or 'Christos' in Greek, hence Jesus 'Christ'). Although some possible candidates had come and gone, none had totally fitted the description.

From these prophecies, the Jews knew the Messiah would be descended from the line of Judah[3] and from King David,[4] that he would be born in Bethlehem[5] and that in some way the region of Galilee would be honoured.[6] There is mention of a virgin bearing a son[7] and the promise of a shepherd, a new David.[8] Yet, these were just a few of the pieces to be joined together ... and had now become ancient prophecies. By the time of what we now call the first century BC, there hadn't been anyone speaking on behalf of God for years and years and years ... In fact, between the last prophetic words God spoke through the prophet Malachi and the appearance of Angel Gabriel to Zechariah at the beginning of Luke's gospel, it was roughly 400 years since the Jews had heard from God.

One of their prophets, Amos, had prophesied a period of silence from the Lord, stating that there would be *'a famine of hearing the words of the LORD ... searching for the word of the LORD, but they will not find it'*[9] But 400 years was an incredibly long time! Can you imagine a silence that long? For us, that's equivalent to going back to the period of the Stuarts, to the reign of James 1 in the 1620s – that's how long it had been since the Jewish nation had heard a prophecy or word from God.

5

God's timing is often very different from ours! As 2 Peter tells us: *'with the Lord a day is like a thousand years, and a thousand years are like a day. The Lord is not slow in keeping his promise, as some understand slowness.'*[10]

But the Jews waited ... and they waited ... and no more prophets appeared. There was no further word from the Lord until not a prophet but an angel appeared. He spoke first to a priest called Zechariah. Then he quietly visited a young woman as she went about her daily chores, saying that the time had come and God's messenger – even better than that, God's very own Son – was on his way, but in a very different manner than anything the Jewish people had imagined. What had been hidden for ages and generations was beginning to be disclosed to the Lord's people ... and it began with Zechariah.

The Advent season reminds us to wait patiently. Some of us are better at waiting than others, but all of us probably struggle to wait a long time for something. We may have periods of silence from God, but we are not abandoned. God is not in a hurry. We need to continue trusting him, even though we may not understand why God, who is outside time, is seeming to delay. God will act in his way and in his time – maybe not in the way we anticipated or requested or even within our hoped-for timescale.

For the next twenty-three days, we will wait to celebrate Christmas and Jesus' first coming, as a baby. But we also wait for another day, which could be tomorrow, or next month, or never in our own lifetime but hundreds of years in the future. We wait for that great day when Jesus will come again in glory, as he has promised.

We have been waiting over five times as long as the Hebrew nation did, without further news or update, for the prophecy of the Lord Jesus' return to be fulfilled. It's so easy to get into a lull, where we allow lethargy to creep in.

As we reflect on how Jesus' coming at Bethlehem fulfilled all the Old Testament prophecies about the Messiah, so we are called to wait patiently for Jesus to fulfil both Old Testament prophecies and New Testament promises. One day he will return to inaugurate the new heaven and the new earth in all its wonder and glory. Let's encourage each other to go on waiting expectantly, however hard this is.

1   Genesis 21:5 cf. Genesis 16:13
2   Exodus 12:40–41, quoted in Acts 7:6
3   Genesis 49:10
4   2 Samuel 7:12–13
5   Micah 5:2
6   Isaiah 9:1
7   Isaiah 7:14
8   Ezekiel 34:23
9   Amos 8:11–12
10 2 Peter 3:8–9

Song: 'O come, O come, Emmanuel' by J.M. Neale

Name to ponder: **'Desire of the nations'** (Haggai 2:7, NKJV)

'The only certainty in the time to come'

Jesus' second coming

> But about that day or hour no one knows, not even the angels in heaven, nor the Son, but only the Father ... So you also must be ready, because the Son of Man will come at an hour when you do not expect him.
>
> MATTHEW 24:36, 44

In 1918 the Spanish flu pandemic killed between 50 and100 million people worldwide – many more than the fatalities of the First World War. It was universal and indiscriminate in its devastation. Some people anticipated that at a certain time in the future this might reoccur. At the beginning of 2007, 'Exercise Winter Willow' was the code name used by the professionals tasked by the Department of Health to simulate a pandemic, based on the influenza virus. The aim was to test what contingency planning was in place in the event of a UK-wide pandemic. Over five thousand people were involved, representing the government, industry and the voluntary sector. A few years later, 'Cygnus', a similar operation with smaller numbers involved, attempted the same exercise.

The intention of being prepared was praiseworthy, but both exercises failed with their insubstantial practical outworkings. Their focus was also restricted to just a flu pandemic. As years went on and economies began to feel the pinch, funding was diverted from contingency planning, since it was no longer considered a priority. However, the coronavirus outbreak, which began in Wuhan at the very end of 2019, killed somewhere in the region of between 3 and 15 million people worldwide, and had lasting effects on many hundreds of thousands of others.

In the same way that preparation for a pandemic slipped down the order of priorities for the government, so the urgency to remember that Jesus will return as he promised can slip down our priority list. We can be so distracted by simply getting through each day. The buzz word bandied around at the time of the worldwide coronavirus pandemic was that it was 'unprecedented'; so will be Jesus' second coming! His return to judge the world – and wrap up history and the universe as we know it – will be unprecedented. No one knows when that day will be, just as the experts in risk management didn't know that the coronavirus pandemic would break out. They were taken by surprise and the stocks of necessary equipment to tackle it weren't available. In our reading today, only God the Father knows the exact timing of when Jesus, the Son of Man, will return. Will we be ready?

When I worked in accident and emergency as a nurse, a key device was a red phone with a distinctive ring. The ambulance staff used this to communicate to the resuscitation team their anticipated time of arrival and the nature of the casualty for which we should prepare. It shot adrenaline through the hearts of the staff on resuscitation duty, and gave warning of a tiny window of preparation time to physically go and be in place the second the patient was rushed through the door.

There will be no phone call or preparation time when Jesus comes again; the warning has already been given. We need to prepare now; there will be no second chances. Jesus will come at a time we do not expect, like a thief in the night.[1] Are we ready?

It is highly likely we will be asked at least once over the next month this potentially irritating question: 'All ready for Christmas?' – a question we may even have been asked at the end of November! Perhaps it can prompt us to think whether, and how, we are preparing our hearts and minds for Jesus' coming again. As we turn our eyes once again to the Christmas story and marvel at the extraordinary, meticulous planning that went into Jesus' first coming, perhaps it can encourage us to remember the equally meticulous planning that has gone into the timing of Jesus' second coming?

[1]   1 Thessalonians 5:2; Revelation 16:15; cf. Matthew 24:43

Song: 'The splendour of a King' by Chris Tomlin

Name to ponder: **'Son of man, coming with the clouds of heaven'** (Daniel 7:13)

4 DECEMBER

'It's all in the timing'

The cosmic spreadsheet

> But when the set time had fully come, God sent his Son, born of a woman, born under the law.
>
> GALATIANS 4:4

Every October, the Literature Festival in Cheltenham draws crowds of around 17,000 people over a ten-day period. The planning is meticulous and people come from far and wide to hear what the many eminent and popular speakers have to say and to listen to their views. Reporters are there to record the events as they happen and their accounts are read nationally, while the many visitors return home with their own stories of the speakers.

Imagine turning up to an advertised event at the festival, arriving at the correct venue at the correct time, only to find the place in complete chaos: there aren't any attendants to open doors and check tickets; the venue is far too small; there are faulty sound and lighting systems so that the speakers can't be heard and their faces can't even be seen at the back ... These things are all important; the details matter. Preparation for an event has to be thorough for it to be deemed successful. Without it there is no point in putting on a festival and paying considerable fees to line up speakers.

It stands to reason that if God is going to send his beloved Son – his only Son – into the world to die for us, he is going to prepare mighty thoroughly. In our reading today, from a letter to a group of churches in modern Turkey, the apostle Paul summarises the first coming of Jesus in a short but very striking way.

First, God has the set the timing for Jesus' birth perfectly. This is no accident of history; nor is it an action taken spontaneously or 'on the hoof' because his purposes for humanity had gone pear-shaped. Jesus' birth happens exactly how it is meant to be and exactly when it is meant to be. It is also exactly where it is meant to be – planned impeccably and accomplished perfectly.

I have often been struck by the fact that the birth of Jesus took place when the known Mediterranean world was under the rule of a Roman emperor, Augustus. People and places from vast areas covering Europe, North Africa and the Middle East were connected by trade routes, common languages (Latin, Greek, Aramaic) and the rule of Roman Law. News could travel quickly and easily as people travelled far and wide on its impressive road network. Communication was therefore easier than ever before. Literacy was also on the increase, with scribes able to record events, then create and copy manuscripts on papyrus.

Secondly, on previous occasions in the Old Testament, God had sent either an angel or a prophet to prepare or communicate significant news. This time he sent his Son. The enormity of that statement is easily lost. Why did God choose to do this? Why not send an angel and make sure people listened? It is because, as we shall think of more in the coming days, only God's One and Only Son could accomplish the work for which he was sent.

Thirdly, God's Son was born of a woman – his Son was to come as a human being, born from a mother's womb. Only in being 'one of us' and living among us could we relate fully to him and he to us. How remarkable that in a world which has often undervalued the status of women (and still does in many places today), God gave, at this set time, a woman the unparalleled privilege of bearing his Son.

Fourthly, God's Son was born under law – under the covenant of Abraham and the law of Moses; born a Jew. In a similar way to its treatment of women, the history of the human race does not often read well in its treatment of the Jewish nation.

I also find it noteworthy that Jesus was born into a nation aware of the ways, character and workings of God, who was worshipped in their restored temple in Jerusalem. So there was already a certain understanding on which to build and to which to relate.

Additionally, the combination of Jewish law and Roman law was very important to the timing of Jesus' coming, so that the accounts of his interrogation, trial and resurrection stand up to scrutiny today. The Jewish law of the time required death for alleged blasphemy or claiming to be the Son of God (which Jesus publicly claimed), while Roman law could execute by crucifixion. Both were important to fulfil the prophecies in the Old Testament of how Jesus would die. Death by burning at the stake as a means of punishment, for example, wouldn't have fulfilled these prophecies. In Jesus' feet (and hands) being nailed to a wooden cross, these prophecies could be seen to be fulfilled.[1]

Cheltenham has a number of annual festivals, but Jerusalem had even more to celebrate throughout the year. The historian Josephus records that at the Passover celebration the number of pilgrims visiting Jerusalem would increase to around 2 million. Thousands of Jews (some whose families had previously been exiled and settled in far-off lands) would travel to worship and then return home. Jerusalem's festivals must have taken some planning!

Yet, amazingly – at just the right time, at that perfectly planned moment in history – God sent his Son to be born of a woman, to be born a Jew, in a backwater of one of the most powerful empires in history. From here Christianity would spread, take root and eventually reach the ends of the earth. God's ways turn human expectations upside down and often challenge our prejudices, our misconceptions and our misguided value systems.

This God can be trusted. He is reliable. He knows what he is doing. May our trust grow this Advent in the God whose timings are perfect for things large and small: from world events affecting us all, to national events affecting some of us, to small events affecting just us. Although we often do not understand his ways or his timings, his will and purposes come to pass at just the right time. He is the Master of all planners and he never makes a mistake.

[1]   John 3:14; Galatians 3:13; cf Genesis 3:15

Song: 'I cannot tell' by W.Y. Fullerton

Name to ponder: **'The Lord will provide / Jehovah Jireh'** (Genesis 22:14)

'The time is set'

The Day will come …

For he has set a day when he will judge the world with justice by the man he has appointed. He has given proof of this to everyone by raising him from the dead.

ACTS 17:31

Yesterday, we were thinking about God's perfect timing in sending his Son to be born of a woman and born a Jew. In our reading today, the doctor Luke, who wrote the book of Acts as well as one of the gospels, recounts a speech given by the apostle Paul in the important ancient city of Athens. Paul is speaking to members of the very respected city council, or Areopagus, whose members were all former city officials. He tells them that God has set another perfectly planned and timed day, one day in the future, when Jesus will return. Given that the Areopagus sometimes met as a law court, they would have been particularly struck by Paul talking of a day in the future when Jesus would preside over his courtroom.

Who will be judged in Jesus' courtroom? Not an individual Athenian for committing a crime, as usually came before the Areopagus, but the whole world, the whole of humanity. We will all one day stand before the judgement seat of King Jesus, and Advent encourages us to think seriously about this. Will we be ready to face him and give account for our lives? How do we feel about that prospect? Daunted, terrified, confident?

How will this judgement be made? Not through the wisdom of mature Athenian citizens, but with complete justice. There will be no bias, no favouritism, no bribery or corruption, but judgement will be made with 100% fairness and justice. There will be no extenuating circumstances or circumstantial evidence, no uncertainties or proving beyond reasonable doubt. The judge's decision will be from all the evidence, and it will be final.

Who could be wise enough to dispense this complete justice? Someone who is innocent of wrongdoing and utterly blameless; someone perfect who does not deserve to die; the only human being in history to be raised from the dead, never to die again, since death could not hold him. One of Jesus' names is 'the Lamb of God' because he offered himself as the perfect sacrifice to bear our sin in our place, just as in the ancient Jewish sacrificial system a pure and spotless lamb was offered as a sacrifice in the temple.[1] Now he is seated as the Lamb upon the throne with all power and authority, and that makes him uniquely qualified to be our Judge – perfect and powerful.[2]

For the Christian believer, the Bible's teaching about Jesus' second coming to judge the world is sobering but need not be terrifying. It drives us to our knees in gratitude before the cross of Christ, where this same Jesus paid the price for human sin – all human sin; our sin; my sin. It leads us to praise and wonder at the resurrection of Christ, which proves that life after death is possible, for he has gone before us. It fills us with wonder that Jesus stands in heaven to plead for us, if we have claimed his death in our place. But more than this, it sends us out to bring this message of hope to those around us. A certain hope, for those who are victims of gross injustices, that their perpetrators will be punished. Hope for a restored relationship with God. Hope that death is not the end. Hope of freedom from all that is evil, from persecution, from grief and pain. Hope of restoration from sickness and disability. If this verse from Acts does not motivate us to tell others about all that Jesus has done through his death and resurrection, then have we really grasped its importance? Why would we keep this good news to ourselves?

May this Advent season see us more committed to prayer for those around us who don't know about the Lord Jesus' sacrifice and resurrection. May we also be more full of praise that God should love the world so much that he sent his Son Jesus into the world as a perfect human specifically to die for us, and that his resurrection from the dead proves that his sacrifice was acceptable to God. Let's pray not only to be more motivated and ready to share this good news but also for opportunities to do so.

1   Exodus 12:5
2   Revelation 5:6; 22:1

Song: 'Before the throne of God above' by Charitie Lees Bancroft and Vikki Cook

Name to ponder: **'Our advocate'** (1 John 2:1)

6 DECEMBER

'One at a time'

Forerunners from times past

He said to them, 'How foolish you are, and how slow to believe all that the prophets have spoken! Did not the Messiah have to suffer these things and then enter his glory?' And beginning with Moses and all the Prophets, he explained to them what was said in all the Scriptures concerning himself.

LUKE 24:25–7

Ouch! None of us likes to be called foolish, and particularly if we really should know better. Luke recalls in his gospel an account of when the resurrected Jesus appears to two of his followers, as they are walking on the road from Jerusalem to Emmaus. Jesus explains to them everything that is written about himself in the Scriptures. What an explanation that must have been to hear! For not only does Jesus interpret the Old Testament, but he reveals to these two followers that it is all about him. What I would give to have overheard that conversation!

Have you ever come across a photo of what at first glance looks like a tree or twig, only to be informed that there is an insect or creature completely camouflaged within it? Initially you couldn't see it, but with renewed insight you wonder how you could possibly have missed it. The Old

Testament is full of anticipation of the Messiah in the form of images, examples, symbols, illustrations and forerunners. It's rich with clues to point us to, and help us to recognise, the Messiah, and in hindsight we can see those clues more clearly placed for us.

What follows are some of my own personal reflections on the clues and pointers I find so amazing. I'm sure many of us wonder which themes, verses and passages Jesus explained to those two disciples. We can never know, of course, but I wonder whether some, or any, of the following were included.

Did they discuss important themes like the temple and sacrificial system, which reminded Jews of their inability to keep God's laws and pointed forward to Jesus' self-sacrifice on the cross once for all?[1] Maybe they also chatted about the Jewish priesthood, which points to an intermediary being necessary between humans and God – who is Jesus, our great High Priest.[2]

In the book of Genesis, we have the account of Abraham, who is told by God to sacrifice his only son Isaac in the region of Moriah. This is the very place where Solomon would build the temple, close to Golgotha where Jesus would be crucified. As Abraham and Isaac are building an altar with firewood, Isaac questions his father where the lamb is for them to sacrifice. Abraham answers that God himself will provide the lamb for the offering.[3] This is a picture of God the Father, who actually went through with offering his beloved only Son as a sacrificial offering for our sin. In Abraham's case, God provides a previously unseen ram to offer instead of Isaac; Jesus would become himself our sacrificial lamb.

Then there's Joseph, living in an alien land as a young man. He was tempted and accused by an influential character of a crime he didn't commit, unjustly sentenced to prison together with two other criminals and later released from jail to the highest office in the land.[4] Here are yet more similarities to Jesus' trial and punishment, resurrection and ascension.

In the book of Exodus, we are introduced to Moses and can see the similarities with Jesus' first months as a baby. Moses is hidden in the bulrushes shortly after his birth, so that he could live; all the other boys of his age are killed by drowning in the Nile under Pharoah's edict. Jesus is taken by his parents to Egypt when King Herod issues an edict that all the baby boys under two in the Bethlehem area are to be killed.[5]

Later in Exodus, instructions are given by Moses to the Israelites about what they must do for the Passover to escape God's judgement on the Egyptians.[6] Once more, this is important for us to understand so that we grasp Jesus being our Passover lamb, with his blood metaphorically daubed over the doorpost of our lives. If we have put our trust in him, God's wrath passes over us.

Moving on to the book of Numbers, it is written that Moses delivers the Israelites in the wilderness from fatal poisonous snakes by making a bronze snake, as instructed by God, and lifting it up on a pole.[7] When anyone bitten by a snake looks at the bronze snake, they live – a wonderful foreshadowing of Jesus being 'lifted' on the cross to enable us to live, if we look to him.

In the book of Ruth, we meet Boaz, a Bethlehemite of the tribe of Judah, who becomes a kinsman-redeemer for Ruth and so provides her with protection and security, as Christ does for us. Boaz agrees to marry Ruth, a widow of a distant relative; he is the most wonderful picture of God's provision of Jesus as a 'husband' to his church (sometimes called his bride). Ruth is from a nation despised by Israel yet Boaz acts in a loving, honourable and respectful manner, providing for her needs. In God's mercy, their child becomes an ancestor of the Lord Jesus.[8]

Then there is the prophet Elisha, another example of a forerunner, who on one occasion feeds 100 people with twenty loaves of bread, with leftovers – a miracle Jesus is to do to a far greater extent, when he feeds 4,000 people.[9]

Finally in my chosen list today comes Jonah, who miraculously spends three days in the belly of a great fish, an account used by Jesus himself to foretell his future death and resurrection on the third day.[10]

There are many other examples, foreshadowing the coming Messiah, and over the next few days, we will look at individual forerunners of God's Messiah Jesus in more detail. My hope is that these examples mentioned today show the amazing range of how God planned, prepared for and foreshadowed his Son. Thank God for the richness of the Old Testament Scriptures!

[1]   Leviticus 4:1 – 6:7; Hebrews 7:26–28; 9:24–26
[2]   Exodus 28:1–2; Hebrews 4:14
[3]   Genesis 22:1–14
[4]   Genesis 39:6–21; 40:2–3; 41:39–44
[5]   Exodus 1:22 – 2:10; Matthew 2:13–16
[6]   Exodus 12:21–8; Hebrews 9:11–12
[7]   Numbers 21:9
[8]   Ruth 4:9–12; Matthew 1:5; Revelation 19:5–9
[9]   2 Kings 4:42–44; Mark 8:1–10
[10]   Jonah 1:17; Matthew 12:40

Song: 'Of the Father's love begotten' by Aurelius C. Prudentius (tr. J.M Neale)

Name to ponder: **'Forerunner'** (Hebrews 6:20)

'A brief history of time'

The genealogy of Jesus

This is the genealogy of Jesus the Messiah, the son of David, the son of Abraham:

Abraham was the father of Isaac,
    Isaac the father of Jacob,
    Jacob the father of Judah and his brothers,
    Judah the father of Perez and Zerah, whose mother was Tamar,
    Perez the father of Hezron,
    Hezron the father of Ram,
    Ram the father of Amminadab,
    Amminadab the father of Nahshon,
    Nahshon the father of Salmon,
    Salmon the father of Boaz, whose mother was Rahab,
    Boaz the father of Obed, whose mother was Ruth,
    Obed the father of Jesse,
    and Jesse the father of King David.
    David was the father of Solomon, whose mother had been Uriah's wife,
    Solomon the father of Rehoboam,
    Rehoboam the father of Abijah,
    Abijah the father of Asa,
    Asa the father of Jehoshaphat,
    Jehoshaphat the father of Jehoram,
    Jehoram the father of Uzziah,

Uzziah the father of Jotham,
Jotham the father of Ahaz,
Ahaz the father of Hezekiah,
Hezekiah the father of Manasseh,
Manasseh the father of Amon,
Amon the father of Josiah,
and Josiah the father of Jeconiah and his
brothers at the time of the exile to Babylon.
After the exile to Babylon:
Jeconiah was the father of Shealtiel,
Shealtiel the father of Zerubbabel,
Zerubbabel the father of Abihud,
Abihud the father of Eliakim,
Eliakim the father of Azor,
Azor the father of Zadok,
Zadok the father of Akim,
Akim the father of Elihud,
Elihud the father of Eleazar,
Eleazar the father of Matthan,
Matthan the father of Jacob,
and Jacob the father of Joseph, the husband of
Mary, and Mary was the mother of Jesus who is
called the Messiah.

MATTHEW 1:1–16

Reading a list like this can cause some people's eyes to glaze over; it's a long, long list of names we mostly don't recognise. For me, this is an incredibly exciting list – and one which could cause some degree of astonishment to its Jewish readers! It spans hundreds of years and contains some very surprising names. But one of the most exciting things is that this genealogy exists. It happened.

There was a time when the existence of so many prophecies about the Messiah coming from the line of Judah could have been a point of extraordinary grief for the Jewish people. They thought the royal line had been wiped out and there was absolutely no way that God's promises could now come true. We will look at that in more detail in a few days' time.

If we were to trace our own family trees in a mere list such as the one above, there would be no mention of the two world wars, as well as other untold tragedies with loss of life causing the tree's branches to veer off in different directions. In a similar way, Matthew's genealogy includes two periods of exile – first when the population in the north of Israel was taken off en masse to Assyria, and later when the people in the south were removed to Babylon. Before those exiles, the Israelites were threatened by a Pharaoh in Egypt (during Moses' time). Then during the exiles, King Ahasuerus (Esther's husband), under the influence of Haman 'the Jew Hater', threatened to exterminate the Jewish race. By the end of this family tree, Judea is under Roman occupation, but again there is no mention of that in the genealogy.

Reading this great long list of names from the beginning of Matthew's gospel gives us a snapshot of the male royal line from the tribe of Judah (the great-grandson of Abraham). Although it lists many kings, careful readers of the Old Testament will note that Jesus' family ancestry also contains characters with important stories behind the names, some of which are very surprising. The honesty of the list is quite refreshing!

When someone rises to prominence in today's world, there is a rush for reporters to 'dish the dirt' and to discredit a squeaky-clean image. One of the wonderful things about this genealogy is its truthfulness. There's no airbrushing here; the skeletons in the cupboard are all in evidence with no holds barred. There are morally flawed people, some women who were non-Jews, and kings that get a bad press in the history books of Kings and Chronicles.

But should we be surprised? Perhaps this list is a big clue as to who God uses, and how he uses them, to fulfil his purposes? Nothing can thwart God's plan. He will always, absolutely accomplish his plans and fulfil promises made a thousand years previously. God often doesn't choose people who look, and are, impressive.[1] He delights to use the underdog, the humble, the nobody, the nameless, the overlooked. He even uses those who reject his lordship. There's no room for boasting in this list. It's transparent and honest.

God's plan was for the human ancestry of his Son to include, especially towards the end of the line, ordinary people like you and me. Joseph, his legal father, was a carpenter by trade, and his mother came from a village in the hills.

It's extremely unusual for any woman to feature in ancient Middle Eastern genealogies, so a first-century Jew reading this list would surely have been struck by the inclusion of four, all of whom were cultural 'outsiders' or 'non-Jews'. So who are these women? Tamar, the mother of Judah's twins Perez and Zerah, was actually a Canaanite and his own son's widow.[2] Eyebrows would surely also have been raised at the mention of Boaz's mother Rahab, who was originally a prostitute from Jericho.[3] Boaz's own wife Ruth was a foreigner from Moab yet became the mother of Obed.[4] Solomon was the son of the great king David by Bathsheba (referred to as 'the wife of Uriah' – a Hittite foreigner), with whom he had committed adultery before ordering her husband's death.[5]

How wonderful and reassuring that women, non-Jews and flawed people are mentioned in Matthew's genealogy as a clue that the gospel of Christ is for male and female, Jew and Gentile, saint and sinner. God's grace is highlighted right from the beginning ... so there is hope for us all.[6]

[1] 1 Corinthians 1:26–9
[2] Genesis 38:1–30
[3] Joshua 2:1–2; 6:25
[4] Ruth 1:4; 4:13–17
[5] 2 Samuel 11:1–27; 12:24–25
[6] Galatians 3:29

Song: 'O come, all you unfaithful' by Bob Kauflin and Lisa Clow

Name to ponder: **'Carpenter's son'** (Matthew 13:55)

8 DECEMBER

'The lion's share of time'

Judah's roots and shoots

Then Jacob called for his sons and said: 'Gather
around so I can tell you what will happen to you
in days to come …

'Judah, your brothers will praise you;
    your hand will be on the neck of your enemies;
    your father's sons will bow down to you.
    You are a lion's cub, Judah;
    you return from the prey, my son.
    Like a lion he crouches and lies down,
    like a lioness – who dares to rouse him?
    The sceptre will not depart from Judah,
    nor the ruler's staff from between his feet,
    until he to whom it belongs shall come
    and the obedience of the nations shall be his.
    He will tether his donkey to a vine,
    his colt to the choicest branch;
    he will wash his garments in wine,
    his robes in the blood of grapes.
    His eyes will be darker than wine,
    his teeth whiter than milk.'

GENESIS 49:1, 8–12

A few days ago we looked at the clues the Jewish nation had been given in looking for the Messiah. One of those was a prophecy that he would come from the line, or tribe, of Judah. Yesterday we zoomed out and looked at Jesus' genealogy, tracing it from his adoptive father Joseph right the way back to Abraham, showing that Jesus was indeed of the line of Judah. Today we will zoom in on an individual man, Judah, to whom these promises were first given.[1]

Today's passage is from the chapter in Genesis where Jacob (Abraham's grandson and Isaac's son) gives his final words, before dying, to each of his twelve sons, reflecting on how they have used their lives so far and predicting their futures. Although Judah is Jacob's fourth son (his first wife Leah had previously given birth to Reuben, Simeon and Levi), he receives a wonderful prophetic blessing from his father, given around a thousand years before Jesus' birth.

So who was Judah? Although he was part of the plot to get rid of their second youngest brother Joseph, Judah is recorded as having more of a conscience than the others. Genesis tells of him urging his brothers to sell Joseph into slavery to some passing Midianites rather than killing him.[2] Years later, Judah promises his father Jacob that he will guarantee the youngest brother Benjamin's safety when he must join his brothers in Egypt – at the insistence of Joseph, who God has now made a very powerful ruler in Egypt, though his brothers don't yet recognise him.[3] This is the family's second visit there to buy food to survive a famine. Finally, Judah offers to remain in place of Benjamin when Joseph sets a further test to see whether his brothers are still the same cheating and deceitful men that tried to destroy him so many years before.[4] Judah's story reveals someone who offered himself as a guarantor of life and safety, and then as a substitute to gain another's freedom: glimmers of what Jesus would come to do.

What can we learn from Jacob's blessing on Judah? It

starts by prophesying that his descendants will become pre-eminent over those of his brothers in the future: *'your brothers will praise you ... your father's sons will bow down to you'.* Some of his descendants will in fact be kings: *'You are a lion's cub, Judah ... The sceptre will not depart from Judah'.* As we saw in Matthew's genealogy, the list of kings does descend from Judah. No doubt this influenced C.S. Lewis to depict Aslan as a lion in his books about *The Chronicles of Narnia.* But Jacob's blessing goes on to narrow its focus to a single descendant, the greatest king: *'he to whom it belongs shall come'.*

How amazing that such detail is given here when we look at the life, death and resurrection of Jesus. We may think of Jesus' triumphal entry riding on a donkey: *'He will tether his donkey to a vine, his colt to the choicest branch.'* We may think of the symbolism of Jesus' death: *'he will wash his garments in wine, his robes in the blood of grapes'.* We can see the significance of Jesus' resurrection and ascension, proclaiming him as the true king before whom one day every knee will bow: *'and the obedience of the nations shall be his'.*

In Revelation, the final book of the New Testament, we read: *'Then one of the elders said to me, "Do not weep! See, the Lion of the tribe of Judah ... has triumphed. He is able to open the scroll and its seven seals."'*[5] This helps us to keep our minds focused on Jesus' second coming as well as his first, as John records his 'revelation' of no one being worthy to open the scroll with seven seals (the opening of which brings about the end of the world) except the Lion of Judah, the Lord Jesus Christ. Only he is worthy, worshipped by the four living creatures, the twenty-four elders and angels numbering thousands upon thousand, and ten thousand times ten thousand! *'Worthy is the Lamb, who was slain, to receive power and wealth and wisdom and strength and honour and glory and praise!'*[6]

1   Judah is both the name of one of Jacob's sons and thence the name of one of the tribes of Israel, which gave its name to a geographical area. When the kingdom of Israel became divided after Solomon's reign, the southern kingdom was known as Judah, while the northern kingdom retained the name Israel. In Jesus' day, the area was known as Judea.

2   Genesis 37:26–27

3   Genesis 43:9; see also Genesis 42

4   Genesis 44:33–34

5   Revelation 5:5–6

6   Revelation 5:12

Song: 'You're the Lion of Judah' by Robin Mark

Name to ponder **'Lion of Judah'** (Revelation 5:5)

'A time to remember'

Son of David

> ... when your days are over and you rest with your ancestors, I will raise up your offspring to succeed you, your own flesh and blood, and I will establish his kingdom ... Your house and your kingdom shall endure for ever, before me your throne shall be established for ever.
>
> 2 SAMUEL 7:12, 16

Delia Owen's murder mystery novel, *Where the Crawdads Sing*, has sold over 18 million copies. On reaching the last chapter, in which the perpetrator was revealed, I found myself compelled to immediately reread the entire novel to pick up the clues I had missed the first time! Knowing the ending helped me to recognise details in the storyline as they were introduced.

Today, as we continue to think about Old Testament forerunners of Jesus, we will look at the promise that the Messiah will be of the line of David, sometimes interchangeably being called *a* or *the* 'Son of David'. It's a theme picked up regularly later in the Bible by Old Testament prophets and deliberately alluded to by New Testament writers.

In today's reading, God states categorically to David (through the prophet Nathan) that there will always be someone from his line on the throne – 'for ever'. Given that it is recorded that God referred to David as a man *'after his own heart'*,[1] the highest possible accolade, it is perhaps of no surprise that God trusted him with some very specific promises.

Centuries later, Luke records the angel Gabriel announcing to Mary that she will have a son, and that the promise of 2 Samuel will be fulfilled in him: *'The Lord God will give him the throne of his father David and he will reign over Jacob's descendants for ever; his kingdom will never end.'*[2]

David had nineteen sons, one of whom, Solomon, was renowned for his wisdom and greatness as he succeeded to the throne of Israel. At first sight, therefore, this prophecy might appear to refer to him, but he – inevitably of course – died, which ruled him out as lasting for ever. As God reveals more to his prophets, a number of qualities and specific actions need to be fulfilled in the descendant of David for him to qualify to be the promised Messiah.

For example, Isaiah prophesies that extraordinary signs would accompany his coming: *'Then will the eyes of the blind be opened, and the ears of the deaf unstopped. Then will the lame leap like a deer, and the mute tongue shout for joy.'*[3]

In Matthew's gospel alone, we read of five times when individuals cry out to Jesus, addressing him as the 'son of David'. Three of these accounts concern blind people, pleading with Jesus to have mercy on them in their affliction, and he restores their sight.[4] On another occasion, when Jesus is asked if he is the Messiah, his answer is: *'Go back ... and report what you hear and see: the blind receive sight, the lame walk, those who have leprosy are cleansed, the deaf hear, the dead are raised, and the good news is proclaimed to the poor.'*[5]

Ezekiel prophesies that God would raise up for his people someone who would be a shepherd like David.[6] Although later a great king (who was figuratively to act as a shepherd to his whole people), David was initially a shepherd boy. He was also gifted with the lyre and poetry. Just under half of the psalms, including the well-known Psalm 23 ('The Lord is My Shepherd'), are poems attributed to him and they reveal his priorities and heartaches. His writing appears so inspired by the Spirit of God that some of his poems have two layers of meaning – both for himself and for a future descendent, whom we now can see is Jesus.[7] In John's gospel, Jesus calls himself 'the good shepherd',[8] who protects his flock from the enemy and is willing to lay down his life for his sheep, just as David did.

Zechariah prophesies that Israel's king will come to them mounted on a donkey.[9] After his three years' ministry, Jesus enters Jerusalem on a colt – at the beginning of the Passover week. The crowds pick palms branches, throwing them and their cloaks on the ground on the route he takes and acknowledging him as the Messiah as they cry out *'Hosanna to the son of David'*.[10]

Zechariah also prophesies that God will pour out on the house of David a spirit of grace, and that the Messiah will die by piercing. He goes on to say that the houses of David, Nathan and Levi, and their wives, together with all the clans, would mourn as one mourns a firstborn.[11] All these prophecies are fulfilled. The gospel writer John confidently states that Jesus was *'full of grace and truth'*.[12] Jesus was descended from two of David's sons: Solomon (through Joseph) and Nathan (through Mary).[13] Not only was Jesus of the line of David, but he was to die by his hands and feet being pierced by nails. John, Zechariah and Elizabeth's only son and of the house of Levi, was to die by beheading shortly before Jesus.

In the last book of the Bible, Revelation, John records words given to him by Jesus himself to demonstrate the authority of what he has been shown: *'I, Jesus, have sent my angel to give you this testimony for the churches. I am the Root and the Offspring of David, and the bright Morning Star.*[14]

Two verses in Psalm 89 give us this beautiful reminder: *'Once for all, I have sworn by my holiness – and I will not lie to David – that his line will continue for ever and his throne endure before me like the sun; it will be established for ever like the moon, the faithful witness in the sky.'*[15] As we look up at the night sky, we can be reminded of the fulfilment of God's great promise that there will always be one on the throne of David; his name is Jesus. He will reign for ever, into eternity, when the light of neither the sun nor the moon will be required, for we will have the light of the Lord God for eternity.[16]

[1]   1 Samuel 13:14; see also Acts 13:22
[2]   Luke 1:32–33
[3]   Isaiah 35:5–6
[4]   Matthew 9:27; 12:22–23; 20:30
[5]   Matthew 11:2–5
[6]   Ezekiel 34:23–24
[7]   See, for example, Psalms 17 and 22
[8]   John 10:11
[9]   Zechariah 9:9
[10] Matthew 21:1–11
[11] Zechariah 12:10–14
[12] John 1:14; see also John 1:17
[13] See Luke 3:23–38 for Jesus' ancestry through Mary's line
[14] Revelation 22:16
[15] Psalm 89:35–37
[16] Revelation 21:23; 22:5

Song: 'Hail to the Lord's anointed' by James Montgomery

Name to ponder: **'Son of David'** (Matthew 15:22)

10 DECEMBER

'In the nick of time'

The line of Judah is saved from extinction

A shoot will come up from the stump of Jesse;
   from his roots a Branch will bear fruit.
The Spirit of the Lord will rest on him –
   the Spirit of wisdom and of understanding,
   the Spirit of counsel and of might,
   the Spirit of the knowledge and fear of the Lord –
   and he will delight in the fear of the Lord.

ISAIAH 11:1–3

And though a tenth remains in the land,
   it will again be laid waste.
But as the terebinth and oak
   leave stumps when they are cut down,
   so the holy seed will be the stump in the land.

ISAIAH 6:13

'The days are coming,' declares the Lord, 'when
I will fulfil the good promise I made to the
people of Israel and Judah.

'In those days and at that time
   I will make a righteous Branch sprout from
   David's line;
   he will do what is just and right in the land.
In those days Judah will be saved
   and Jerusalem will live in safety.

> **This is the name by which it will be called:**
> **The Lord Our Righteous Saviour.'**
>
> JEREMIAH 33:14–16

In September 2023, there was outrage when the sycamore gap tree on Hadrian's Wall in Northumbria was felled overnight in an act of vandalism. Aged about 150 years, it had been used over the years in films and was the subject of many a photograph. Its illegal felling left only a bleak stump exposed in the ground. Of course, it is hoped that a shoot will grow out of it, but there will not be another mature tree there in the lifetime of this generation.

Isaiah's two passages speak powerfully of a 'stump' producing a shoot, even when the tree looks to have been cut down and totally destroyed. Jeremiah prophesies in a similar way that a branch will come from the line of David to bring salvation to Israel. But at one point in history it seemed a very close call …

I recently came across the story of the Smith family, a family of six boys born to Margaret and John Smith in Barnard Castle, County Durham. Together with their father, all the brothers signed up to fight in the First World War. Within only two years, between September 1916 and July 1918, five of the sons were killed on the battlefields of northern France and Belgium. The local vicar's wife was so concerned for this family's distress that she wrote on their behalf to Queen Mary, George V's wife. Drawing her attention to this situation, she requested that the youngest brother be granted an official discharge to ensure that the Smiths had one surviving son. Her request was granted and Wilfred was indeed discharged. On Remembrance Sunday 2018, thirty of his descendants, spanning four generations, gathered to lay a wreath. They quoted the words that had brought him back: 'to carry on the line'.

As I have alluded to previously, there was a time when it was thought that the royal line of Judah had been destroyed for ever. The second book of Kings tells an account of Queen Athaliah, who in her fury at her own son King Ahaziah being killed, *'proceeded to destroy the whole royal family'* in an attempt to seize the throne for herself.[1] Unbeknown to her, however, God places Jehosheba, her son's sister (and a priest's wife), in the right place at the right time. Jehosheba grabs her nephew, the toddler Joash, who is the only remaining person of the royal line of Judah. She hides him in a safe room in the temple, whose existence is only known to a handful of people. Being a priest's wife had its advantages! The boy Joash remains with his wet nurse for six years, hidden from Queen Athaliah.

To everyone else, the line of Judah appeared to have been completely and utterly severed. The tree had been felled! For the next seven years there must have been despair that God had forgotten his promise that a king would rule from the line of Judah for ever. But from the stump emerged a shoot, as promised, albeit one very young indeed – Joash was seven years old when he was proclaimed king. In time, though, the tree blossomed once more. Indeed Joash reigned for forty years, and the seed passed on through his son, Amaziah.

God's plans are often realised in unexpected ways. This nameless wet nurse was used by God to look after Joash. We have seen this same theme previously. God delights to use the nobodies, the nameless, the everyday folk to achieve his purposes.

It seems to me that God's plans also often 'go down to the wire'. Around our world today, some of our brother and sister Christians face terrible persecution. I think particularly of those in North Korea. If their faith is discovered by the authorities, they face atrocious conditions in labour camps or instant murder, and it's highly likely that their whole family will be taken too. Extraordinarily these believers do not ask that we pray for their freedom from persecution, but that they would stand firm in their faith in the Lord Jesus, who gave his life for them. Let's remember to pray for them.

We may sometimes feel as though we are a remnant, but God will never allow his people to be eradicated. He will achieve his purposes in his timing and in his way. The zeal of the Lord will accomplish this!

1   2 Kings 11:1–3

Song: 'All hail the power of Jesus' name' by Edward Perronet and John Rippon

Name to ponder: **'Root of David'** (Revelation 5:5)

'The time is coming'

Meet Zechariah and Elizabeth

In the time of Herod king of Judea there was
a priest named Zechariah, who belonged to
the priestly division of Abijah; his wife
Elizabeth was also a descendant of Aaron.
Both of them were righteous in the sight of
God, observing all the Lord's commands and
decrees blamelessly. But they were childless
because Elizabeth was not able to conceive,
and they were both very old.

LUKE 1:5–7

Family history needn't define us, but it may well influence
our thinking and perception of life. Maybe there are specific
people who have been influential in our past or in the lives of
previous generations, or there have been significant events
from our family tree narrated down the years.

Zechariah and Elizabeth, an elderly couple, lived in the
hill country of the region of Judea. This was just over the
valley but at a convenient distance from the hustle and
bustle of Jerusalem, where Zechariah still worked as a priest
in the temple. They could look back at their family history
over hundreds of years and read all about it in some depth,
since it had been chronicled in detail in the Torah, the
Jewish holy book. They could trace their line right back to
Moses' brother Aaron, because (as with all twelve tribes)

meticulous details were kept of the line descending from Levi, which was the line of priests.

The lives of their ancestors, Aaron and Moses, were full of memorable events. These included incidences of the Lord using their staffs (wooden poles) in a supernatural way.[1] One such astonishing miracle concerned a staff with Aaron's name etched on the almond wood, at a time when Aaron's authority had been challenged by the Israelites wandering in the desert. Twelve staffs – one from each of the tribes of Israel – had been placed, at God's command, in the Tent of Meeting overnight. God had stated that the staff of his chosen leader would sprout. The following morning eleven of the staffs were exactly the same, but Aaron's staff alone had totally transformed, overflowing with life. It was sprouting not just leaves, but blossom and even ripe almonds![2] What an extravagant way to illustrate, without doubt, God's blessing on Aaron's priestly authority. This staff was then kept, as instructed, as a tangible reminder to the Israelites in the Ark of the Covenant.[3]

Sometimes in a conversation or written paragraph, just by the tone of voice or phrasing, we can sense that there's a 'but' coming. And so it is with Luke's account of this couple in today's reading. The elderly priest Zechariah is a highly honoured man. Not only is he a priest but his wife, Elisabeth, is a priest's daughter, also descended from Aaron. The privilege of being a priest is a hereditary one, but Zechariah has no one to succeed him because the couple have been unable to have children. Elizabeth is barren. That word is blunt and hides all manner of sadness. They have, no doubt, prayed for the gift of children for years, but this particular privilege has not been granted. Elizabeth's body is dead as far as reproduction is concerned. Her biological clock isn't even still ticking; it stopped years before.

It might be glibly commented 'what a shame' their

situation is. That would be to hugely underestimate that, for a godly couple in that culture, their shame was literal and immense. Luke is at pains to record that they were both 'righteous', yet the Scriptures categorically state that if God's people obeyed him, he would *bless the fruit of your womb*[4]. While Zechariah and Elizabeth have been obedient, God hasn't blessed them with children ... and now time has run out, or so it seems. God might have bought life to a dead wooden staff hundreds of years ago for Aaron, but he hasn't given them life in the form of a child. Many of their contemporaries probably even have grandchildren by this time. Zechariah and Elizabeth know very well about God's blessing on Sarai, Abraham's wife,[5] and Samson's mother,[6] and Hannah, the mother of Samuel,[7] all of whom bore children after previously being barren. However, that hasn't been their experience, and it is unlikely they are expecting anything so incredible to happen to them now.

But God, in his perfect timing, plans that the lot should fall to Zechariah to enter the Holy Place, separated by a colossal curtain from the Holy of Holies, to offer the twice-daily incense. Zechariah's priestly division (of Abijah, a priest in the time of King David[8]) is only 'on duty' for a week, twice a year. Therefore entering the Holy Place is a once-in-a-lifetime opportunity that doesn't necessarily fall to every priest, there being a great many of them. But it is no coincidence that Zechariah has been chosen, and in this particular year, after many, many years as a priest. While Zechariah is in that room, alone with God himself, God has a very significant announcement to make to him.

Unbeknown to Zechariah and Elizabeth, their prayers for a child have been heard in the courts of heaven itself, and the answer for them has been 'wait' rather than 'no'. God delights in impossible situations, particularly when they reveal his glory and his plan. He has something immensely special in store for these two godly people. God's timings are so often not ours. He has a meticulous, intricate, detailed plan.

Maybe we found it easy to start off in the Christian life with enthusiasm. However, as dashed hopes or frustrations step in and dreams are not fulfilled, trust is much harder to maintain and nurture. Zechariah and Elizabeth were in the late chapters of their lives and had known significant disappointment, but our passage tells us that they were still righteous and walking blamelessly before God.

We may not have any particularly inspiring stories in our family tree, but if we belong to the Lord and have been adopted into his family, we have a treasure trove of factual stories to inspire us – the wonders he has done in the past for his people. These can be used to increase our faith that our God can do absolutely anything.[9] Do we take time to remember the numerous ways the Lord has acted in our lives and those around us? Do we talk about these things to others to encourage them in their faith?

As part of a royal priesthood,[10] we have the privilege of being able to go directly into the Lord's presence at anytime, anywhere, to offer prayers for ourselves and for others. Do we persevere in prayer, or give up after a few days or weeks? Perseverance is highly valued in the Scriptures.[11] We could consider finding someone else to meet with regularly to pray through things on our hearts long-term. Perhaps we could reread passages to inspire us and increase our vision of God? Are we able to recall scripture, ponder it and relate its relevance to our daily lives? We could even start learning a few verses by heart.

Finally, do we believe that God's timing is always perfect? We might not see that about things that happen to us until years later, and maybe never at all, but it is a lesson for us from this extraordinary event in the lives of Zechariah and Elizabeth.

1   See, for example, Exodus 4:1–5; 7:8–10; Numbers 20:10–11
2   Numbers 17:1–11
3   Hebrews 9:4
4   Deuteronomy 7:12–13
5   Genesis 18:10–14; 21:1–3
6   Judges 13
7   1 Samuel 1:1–20
8   1 Chronicles 24:10
9   Ephesians 3:20
10 Peter 2:9
11 See, for example, 1 Timothy 6:12; Hebrews 10:36

Song: 'Remember' by Lauren Daigle

Name to ponder: **'The Lord God Almighty'** (Revelation 4:8)

'Predictable times'

Zechariah and Daniel: the backstory

I, Daniel, understood from the Scriptures, according to the word of the Lord given to Jeremiah the prophet, that the desolation of Jerusalem would last seventy years ...

While I was speaking and praying ... Gabriel, the man I had seen in the earlier vision, came to me in swift flight about the time of the evening sacrifice. He instructed me and said to me, 'Daniel, I have now come to give you insight and understanding ...

'Seventy "sevens" [or weeks] are decreed for your people and your holy city to finish transgression, to put an end to sin, to atone for wickedness, to bring in everlasting righteousness, to seal up vision and prophecy and to anoint the Most Holy Place. Know and understand this: From the time the word goes out to restore and rebuild Jerusalem until the Anointed One, the ruler, comes, there will be seven "sevens."'

DANIEL 9:1–2, 20–22, 24–25

Long-term friends, or those from childhood, know us and our family history well. Perhaps they have also heard the same narratives, read the same books and heard the same opinions, all influencing their own thinking. They understand where we are coming from and why we might think as we do.

But all we know about Zechariah is the information in Luke 1, which we read yesterday. We know that Zechariah was a priest and his wife Elizabeth was the daughter of a priest. They would have been privileged to grow up with a wealth of opportunity to hear of the riches in God's word, surrounded by godly people pondering and discussing the Scriptures. They had the opportunity for inside-out knowledge of the history and prophecies of the Old Testament. Priests could only come from the clan of Levi,[1] who were descendants of Aaron and his sons, but this was a privilege granted to many – there was no shortage of priests. When on duty in Jerusalem, the priests would have slept in the chamber of the hearth in the temple. At other times they lived scattered throughout Judah, transcribing Scripture and teaching from it, being fully literate. Synagogues were common in most towns and here the scrolls of Scripture would be regularly read every sabbath to the gathered townsfolk.[2] So let's zoom in and look at our passage above, one of the prophecies Daniel was given, which surely would have influenced Zechariah's thinking.

Daniel was a godly Jew from a noble family, who, when young, was among those exiled from Judah to Babylon[3] – located in present-day Iraq, south of Baghdad. This happened around 600 years before Jesus was born. God gave Daniel a gift of interpreting dreams and visions, which was at times a heavy responsibility to bear.[4] He was able to advise two kings in the light of these interpretations,[5] but always fully acknowledged God and not himself as 'the revealer of mysteries'.[6]

By the time of the Persian king Darius (after Persia

conquered Babylon in 539 BC), Daniel has become a high-ranking government official. Now an elderly man, he has been pondering over the beautiful promises in the book of Jeremiah, concerning the end of the Jewish exile.[7]

We see Daniel praying for the restoration of Israel, perhaps calculating that the seventy years prophesied by Jeremiah must almost be complete. While he is doing this, he is visited by the angel Gabriel (appearing like a man), who comes to interpret a vision that Daniel himself has seen. Gabriel, knowing that Daniel has been pondering Jeremiah's prophecy, tells him that: *'As soon as you began to pray, a word went out, which I have come to tell you, for you are highly esteemed.'*[8]

Gabriel's words in the reading above, including the mention of 'seventy "sevens" [or weeks]', are rather enigmatic (as are many of the visions in the book of Daniel!). But they point to a return home from exile, and a distressing time of unrest before Jerusalem is rebuilt. Gabriel then reveals to Daniel that an 'anointed' Prince will come.

Daniel receives this message at what would have been 'the time of the evening sacrifice' at the temple in Jerusalem, even though he is now far away in Babylon. We know that throughout his life, Daniel made a priority of kneeling to pray three times a day from his upstairs window,[9] which faced in the direction of Jerusalem. I think we could learn a significant principle from this dependence on God for every aspect of our lives. Do we have the habit of daily committing ourselves into his hands? Do we lay before him the cares and concerns on our hearts and minds? Do we try to spend time simply in his presence, adoring and praising him for who he is and thanking him for what he has done? The Advent season is a good time to embed (or re-embed) this practice in our daily lives.

At the temple there had been two specific times of sacrifice each day,[10] and the evening one was at three o'clock. At each sacrifice, it was customary to burn incense to symbolise the prayers of the people rising to heaven. Gabriel had visited Daniel following on from his evening time of prayer. His next recorded visit, centuries later, is to Zechariah. As recorded in Luke's gospel, Zechariah, another righteous man, makes one of the daily offerings of sacrifice and burns incense in the now rebuilt temple.

In naming Gabriel, Luke deliberately seems to be asking his readers to make the connection with this passage from the book of Daniel, where a Messianic figure is prophesied. We will consider Gabriel's announcement to Zechariah tomorrow.

[1] Numbers 1:47–54; 18:6
[2] Luke 4:20–21
[3] Daniel 1:3–7
[4] Daniel 8:27
[5] Daniel 2:25–45; 4:19–27 (for King Nebuchadnezzar); 5:13–28 (for King Belshazzar)
[6] Daniel 2:29
[7] Daniel 9:1–2; Jeremiah 29:10–14
[8] Daniel 9:23
[9] Daniel 6:10
[10] Exodus 29:38–43

Song: 'Standing on the promises' by Russell Kelso Carter

Name to ponder: **'Christ'** – meaning, 'the Anointed One' (1 John 4:2)

'Ahead of one's time'

Gabriel visits Zechariah

Once when Zechariah's division was on duty and he was serving as priest before God, he was chosen by lot, according to the custom of the priesthood, to go into the temple of the Lord and burn incense. And when the time for the burning of incense came, all the assembled worshippers were praying outside.

Then an angel of the Lord appeared to him, standing at the right side of the altar of incense. When Zechariah saw him, he was startled and was gripped with fear. But the angel said to him: 'Do not be afraid, Zechariah; your prayer has been heard. Your wife Elizabeth will bear you a son, and you are to call him John. He will be a joy and delight to you, and many will rejoice because of his birth, for he will be great in the sight of the Lord. He is never to take wine or other fermented drink, and he will be filled with the Holy Spirit even before he is born. He will bring back many of the people of Israel to the Lord their God. And he will go on before the Lord, in the spirit and power of Elijah, to turn the hearts of the parents to their children and the disobedient to the wisdom of the righteous – to make ready a people prepared for the Lord.'

Zechariah asked the angel, 'How can I be sure of this? I am an old man and my wife is well on in years.'

The angel said to him, 'I am Gabriel. I stand in the presence of God, and I have been sent to speak to you and to tell you this good news. And now you will be silent and not able to speak until the day this happens, because you did not believe my words, which will come true at their appointed time.'

Meanwhile, the people were waiting for Zechariah and wondering why he stayed so long in the temple. When he came out, he could not speak to them. They realised he had seen a vision in the temple, for he kept making signs to them but remained unable to speak.

When his time of service was completed, he returned home. After this his wife Elizabeth became pregnant and for five months remained in seclusion. 'The Lord has done this for me,' she said. 'In these days he has shown his favour and taken away my disgrace among the people.'

LUKE 1:8–25

The planning for King Charles' coronation took months of painstaking preparation. For many individuals, such as Penny Mordaunt, whose roles as Lord President of the Privy Council and Leader of the House of Commons were to be in the limelight, a great deal of preparation was necessary. How and where she stood, what she held, what she wore, every detail and timing had to be taken into consideration.

For Zechariah, too, as the chosen priest for this particular occasion, the preparation would have been thorough. The spotlight would have been on him for this greatest honour of his life – presenting the incense offering to God in the Holy

Place during one of the daily sacrifices in the temple in Jerusalem.

On the day itself, Zechariah will have performed various purification rituals and donned specific clothing.[1] A lamb will have been offered as a sacrifice to atone for the sins of the people. He will have ascended the impressive steps, gone through the arch and entered the Holy Place (the room separated from the Holy of Holies by an immense, heavy curtain) to offer incense on the altar.

Meanwhile the people outside in the outer court will have been praying and waiting to see the smoke from the incense rise up (indicating that the prayers of the people have been heard and the sacrifice accepted). They will have been also waiting to hear the trumpets signal Zechariah's exit from the Holy Place. This will be the signal to start singing and a blessing will be pronounced. But the people wait and wait... The trumpets don't sound. As they shuffle around and time goes on, they must be beginning to wonder what the hold-up is: has the elderly priest been struck dead? But Zechariah has not been struck dead; he has been struck dumb.

The angel appears to the right of the altar in the Holy Place, terrifying Zechariah. He says that Zechariah's prayer for a child has been heard and his wife will bear a boy, whom they must name 'John' – and what a child he will be! When Zechariah questions this message, the angel tells him that his name is Gabriel and that he stands in the presence of God.

This message that God sends Gabriel to give to Zechariah, hundreds of years after his visit to Daniel, is that *the* pivotal event in history is shortly to happen. His Son is coming into the world. It will be so significant that the whole dating system of world events will be in reference to it, and Zechariah's son is to have the privilege to prepare people for the arrival of the Messiah.

Zechariah is to name his son John (which means 'God is

gracious'). John will give considerable joy to those around him, being a longed-for child. But the much more significant statement is that he will be 'great in the sight of the Lord' and 'filled with the Holy Spirit', even while still in the womb! His mandate will be like the great Old Testament prophet Elijah before him: to prepare people for the Messiah's arrival.[2]

But we are told that on hearing this news, initially Zechariah doesn't believe Gabriel's message. So he is struck dumb because of his unbelief (and quite possibly deaf too, since they had to sign questions to him until after Elizabeth gives birth).[3] Having nine months to ponder things in his silent world, Zechariah might well have recalled Gabriel's visit to Daniel that we looked at yesterday. He perhaps noted that Gabriel's message was again at the time of sacrifice and of future events, specifically that an Anointed One would come at some point when Israel was restored.

Zechariah has been offering prayers on behalf of the people. In God's amazing timing, two prayers are answered: the corporate prayer of the gathered congregation in the temple that day (and over the preceding centuries) for the Messiah to come, alongside the private prayer over the years for a child for Zechariah and his wife Elizabeth. God's planning is extraordinarily intricate.

Zechariah would also have had plenty of time to ponder (as we did two days ago) that God can do the impossible, bringing life out of what is dead. Just as God made Aaron's rod blossom all those years ago, so he was going to enable Elizabeth's post-menopausal womb, which by itself was unable to kindle life and bring it into fruition, to do just that.

Is it fitting that Zechariah is struck dumb? It strikes me that as a priest, he has the privilege of speaking and explaining God's word to the people. If he doesn't have a grasp of God's purposes and greatness, how can his words inspire others?

51

Perhaps, among the worshippers gathered in the temple courts that day, there are some others doing a great deal of pondering of their own – the devout and righteous Jerusalem-dweller Simeon, who we know is praying for *'the consolation of Israel'*[4] (meaning that God will come and rescue his people), and Anna, who *'never left the temple'*.[5]

At a time when no one has heard anything 'new' from the Lord for years, what inestimable joy Gabriel's words to Zechariah should have generated! He's coming! The Messiah is on his way!

[1] Exodus 39:27–31
[2] Malachi 4:5
[3] Luke 1:62–63
[4] Luke 2:25
[5] Luke 2:37

Song: 'Prepare ye the way of the Lord' by Stephen Schwartz

Although 'of an era' and 'niche', this snippet from the musical *Godspell* captures the essence of the infectious, exuberant, overwhelming joy this good news about the Messiah's imminent arrival brings.

Name to ponder: **'The Lord Creator'** (Isaiah 40:28)

14 DECEMBER

'Immaculate timing'

Mary

In the sixth month of Elizabeth's pregnancy,
God sent the angel Gabriel to Nazareth, a town
in Galilee, to a virgin pledged to be married to a
man named Joseph, a descendant of David. The
virgin's name was Mary. The angel went to her
and said, 'Greetings, you who are highly
favoured! The Lord is with you.'

Mary was greatly troubled at his words and
wondered what kind of greeting this might be.
But the angel said to her, 'Do not be afraid,
Mary, you have found favour with God. You will
conceive and give birth to a son, and you are to
call him Jesus. He will be great and will be
called the Son of the Most High. The Lord God
will give him the throne of his father David, and
he will reign over Jacob's descendants for ever;
his kingdom will never end.'

'How will this be,' Mary asked the angel,
'since I am a virgin?'

The angel answered, 'The Holy Spirit will
come on you, and the power of the Most High
will overshadow you. So the holy one to be born
will be called the Son of God. Even Elizabeth
your relative is going to have a child in her old

age, and she who was said to be unable to
conceive is in her sixth month. For no word from
God will ever fail.'
'I am the Lord's servant,' Mary answered. 'May your
word to me be fulfilled.' Then the angel left her.

LUKE 1:26–38

Have you ever received an email that announces that you've been chosen for some special gift or experience? You know that whoever sent it doesn't actually know anything about you; a computer has just made an impersonal, random selection from millions of emails ... People have become more wise to this now, but some are still hoodwinked.

Not so with Mary. She is no random selection. God has specifically chosen her and knows that, out of everyone, she is the one whose heart and track record are most suited to bearing his Son.

So, what do we know about Mary? Although it is thought that Luke recounts this episode from hearing Mary's own testimony (he bases his gospel on 'eye-witness accounts'[1]), he documents little about her background. Her name, Mary, is a common derivative of Miriam, the name of Moses' sister. We know very little about her immediate family, although there is mention of a sister.[2] At the time of Gabriel's visit, she is living in Nazareth, a village with a population of probably under 500 people, and located in a basin surrounded by hills in Galilee. Nazareth is viewed as one of those 'why would you want to live there?' places that noses are turned up against.[3] We assume she is in her mid-to-late teens simply because that was the usual age for betrothal in those times, and we know that she is engaged to be married to Joseph, a carpenter, a godly man also of the lineage of David.[4]

The timing of Gabriel's visit is perfect. The fact that Mary is officially engaged to Joseph means that a binding commitment (in that culture) has already been made. At the same time, because the marriage has not yet taken place, its consummation has not either.[5] Nonetheless, Joseph still chose to remain totally committed to Mary, providing the necessary support for someone still so young.

Yesterday we read that, six months earlier, God sent Gabriel to tell Zechariah that his wife Elizabeth would conceive the forerunner of the Messiah. Now God sends Gabriel to visit Mary, a relative of Elizabeth, to announce the Messiah's birth. We don't know where this second encounter took place. It's not in the temple or in Jerusalem (in contrast to Gabriel's visit to Zechariah), or during a special festival or on the Sabbath. Gabriel comes from outside time to a sleepy, little, insignificant village, while everyone is quietly going about their daily lives. That fits so often with God's ways!

Gabriel appears in an extremely unthreatening manner, reassuring Mary, who inevitably is initially alarmed. Luke's account (written for someone called 'Theophilus', perhaps a respected Roman) is in stark contrast to the Greco-Roman contemporary mythological stories he would have been familiar with, of gods forcibly seducing humans and impregnating them.

The gentleness and respect of Gabriel's attitude is emphasised very clearly. Gabriel tells Mary that she has found favour with God, she will conceive and give birth to a son, and that the child will be given the throne of his ancestor King David and will reign for ever. It's not until Mary asks for more information that she is told that this child will be born of God, not through Joseph. She doesn't laugh, like Abraham's infertile wife, Sarah, at the impossibility of it all.[6] Nor does she disbelieve it, as we saw Zechariah did, when told his barren wife was to bear a son. She doesn't understand it, but her attitude, as we shall explore more in the next day or two, is just like her son's will be in due course: *'yet not my will, but yours be done.'*[7]

Right from the start, God establishes that there will not be any privileges or strings pulled for his Son, or indeed for his earthly parents. By coming to earth and stepping into our world, Jesus is going to utterly humble himself, and so everything about his entrance will reflect that. He will be born to humble people, and into insignificance and poverty rather than advantage and privilege. This will turn upside down the world's priorities. No one will be too poor or so disadvantaged that they can't relate to Jesus, nor be able to assert that he doesn't understand their situation or experiences. There's a pub in Milton Combe, near Yelverton in Devon, called The Who'd Have Thought It Inn. That name just about sums up the monumental difference between God's plans for his Son's entry into the world and how we would have expected him to accomplish it.

Here are two final thoughts. First, when Mary becomes pregnant with Jesus, it is following a very quiet encounter. When the Spirit descends on Jesus at his baptism, it's as a dove.[8] When he descends on the believers at Pentecost, it's with tongues of fire and a noisy wind.[9] In the past, God descended on Mount Sinai with thunder, lightning, very loud trumpet blasts, clouds and smoke.[10] When Jesus returns, everyone will know and there will be no mistaking it.[11] But as the Holy Spirit overshadows Mary in Jesus' first coming to earth, all is unnoticed and peaceful. Secondly, this is the same Holy Spirit who hovered over the face of the waters, as God brought creation into being.[12] How awesome is that …

1   Luke 1:1–4
2   John 19:25
3   John 1:45–46
4   Matthew 1:18–19
5   Matthew 1:25
6   Genesis 18:12
7   Luke 22:42
8   Matthew 3:16; Luke 3:22
9   Acts 2:1–3
10   Exodus 19:16–20
11   Matthew 24:29–31
12   Genesis 1:2

Song: 'Breath of heaven' by Amy Grant

Name to ponder: **'Son of the Most High'** (Luke 1:32)

'A leap in time'

Elizabeth and Mary

At that time Mary got ready and hurried to a
town in the hill country of Judea, where she
entered Zechariah's home and greeted
Elizabeth. When Elizabeth heard Mary's
greeting, the baby leaped in her womb, and
Elizabeth was filled with the Holy Spirit. In a
loud voice she exclaimed: 'Blessed are you
among women, and blessed is the child you will
bear! But why am I so favoured, that the mother
of my Lord should come to me? As soon as the
sound of your greeting reached my ears, the
baby in my womb leaped for joy. Blessed is she
who has believed that the Lord would fulfil his
promises to her!'

LUKE 1:39–45

Who do you go to when you have a private conundrum and
urgently need wise counsel? Perhaps you might choose a
person who has been through a similar experience and who
will give godly counsel with wise understanding of God's
ways and workings?

Mary has just received some earth-shattering news. She, a
young, betrothed virgin, is to bear the child of the Most
High God. Who can she trust to talk to when there could be

possible misunderstandings about the pregnancy? She could be stoned for becoming pregnant before marriage. And how is she going to explain this to Joseph and her family, let alone to the local villagers?

Fortunately, God is a step ahead in ensuring that Gabriel also informs Mary that her elderly relative Elizabeth is pregnant too, as a result of God's extraordinary intervention! It is highly likely therefore that Elizabeth will understand her predicament and rejoice with her in this surprising privilege; more than that, Mary can talk to Elizabeth privately and take time to process this astonishing news.

And so, Mary hastily travels south to visit Elizabeth, who is by now around six months pregnant. Elizabeth greets Mary with enormous joy (and humility, since culturally the older woman deserved the greater respect from the younger). Elizabeth instantly discerns through the Holy Spirit that Mary has conceived the Lord, the One who will redeem Israel. Her own baby, John, starts leaping around for joy in her womb and making his presence felt. What a surprise for Elizabeth that Mary already knows of her own unexpected pregnancy! The two women wonder and rejoice together at the huge blessings they have been so privileged to receive.

Elizabeth is able to be a tremendous encouragement to Mary: she understands and totally believes her story; she loves the Lord as Mary does; she is wise in her counsel; and she greets Mary so positively, unlike the scorn and slander Mary probably expects from others. Nor is there an inkling of any jealously in Elizabeth, but quite the opposite: she shows genuine humility and appreciation of the superior blessing that God has given to her younger relative Mary.

Meanwhile, Zechariah is still dumb, following his own encounter with the angel Gabriel and his initial refusal to accept what he had been told. We can only wonder what he makes of Mary's visit, although presumably Mary's news will have helped fill in some of the gaps of the story for the elderly couple. As a priest steeped in the Scriptures, perhaps Zechariah is able to reflect on passages like this from the last Old Testament book: *"'I will send my messenger, who will prepare the way before me. Then suddenly the Lord you are seeking will come to his temple; the messenger of the covenant, whom you desire, will come," says the* LORD *Almighty.'*[1]

Today modern medicine greatly increases successful birthrates; in those days childbirth was far more uncertain. Yet Elizabeth and Mary both know that they are going to safely deliver boys, that one will pave the way for the other and even the names God wishes their sons to be given.

Elizabeth feels highly favoured to be visited by Mary, just as Mary is 'highly favoured' to be chosen by God.[2] While we were not part of God's plan for the coming of his Son into the world, nevertheless we too are highly favoured to be chosen by him, to have received the favour of him *'who has blessed us in the heavenly realms with every spiritual blessing in Christ'*.[3] Do we have the humility to wonder at this, or have we become accustomed to it and lost our sense of awe? Do we realise how favoured we are that the Spirit of the Lord Jesus lives in us? We are his chosen people, instructed to *'declare the praises of him who called you out of darkness into his wonderful light'*.[4]

Elizabeth and Mary are a great encouragement to each other. Is there anyone we could be getting alongside to encourage and with whom we might share our love of the Lord? Do we speak of our answers to prayer and the way the Lord is working in our lives? Elizabeth is also wonderfully humble. Is there a lesson in humility for us to learn here? Elizabeth, at her advanced age, is unlikely to see what her son will become, yet what faith she shows in the promises of God. Is there a lesson in faith for us to learn here? Mary is young with a simple, accepting, yet solid faith and total trust. Elizabeth is old with a wealth of faith-tested circumstances, wisdom and knowledge. How lovely to have an example of both women.

It seems to me that Elizabeth's encounter with Jesus in Mary's womb is as extraordinary as Mary Magdalene seeing Jesus resurrected from the dead and crying out: *'I have seen the Lord!'*[5] Is the miracle of the incarnation any less wonderful and worthy of joy and praise than the miracle of the resurrection? How amazing too that John the Baptist, unable to see for himself the resurrected Lord Jesus, leapt for joy at the incarnate Lord Jesus even from Elizabeth's womb! Have we truly grasped the magnitude of the fact that Jesus is God's Son come to earth in human form?

[1]   Malachi 3:1
[2]   Luke 1:28
[3]   Ephesians 1:3
[4]   1 Peter 2:9
[5]   John 20:18

Song: 'Mary did you know?' by Mark Lowry

Name to ponder: **'El Chuwl – The God who gave you birth'** (Isaiah 43:1)

'It's all in the timing'

Mary's testimony

And Mary said,

My soul glorifies the Lord,
  and my spirit rejoices in God my Saviour,
  for he has been mindful
  of the humble state of his servant.
From now on all generations will call me blessed,
  for the Mighty One has done great things for me –
  holy is his name.
His mercy extends to those who fear him,
  from generation to generation.
He has performed mighty deeds with his arm;
  he has scattered those who are proud in their
  inmost thoughts.
He has brought down rulers from their thrones
  but has lifted up the humble.
He has filled the hungry with good things
  but has sent the rich away empty.
He has helped his servant Israel,
  remembering to be merciful
  to Abraham and his descendants for ever,
  just as he promised to our fathers.

LUKE 1:46–54

We've all seen news clips of people winning the lottery, or a seat in an election, or receiving excellent exam results: people so full of surprise that they burst out in excitement. They are so caught in the moment that they release the emotions of their heart.

As Mary visits her cousin Elizabeth, she is so overwhelmed with joy and astonishment that she simply erupts with delight. In fact, she overflows with language describing what an extraordinary honour she has received. God's choosing of her to be integral to the unfolding of his plans leads her to feel incredibly humble. Her profusion of words reveals the genuineness of her heart, extolling God for his greatness and faithfulness in bringing to fruition his promise to Abraham, and sharing with her something of how this age-old mystery will come about. Her song, or testimony, has been sung down the centuries. It is now known as the 'Magnificat' because, quite simply, she magnifies God in her praises.

Mary's words seem to bubble up from within her, combining her reverence for the Lord and her knowledge of his character with the way he has worked in the past and her understanding of what he has recently revealed will happen to her. These words beautifully fulfil the exhortation to *'Glorify the LORD with me; let us exalt his name together.'*[1] Perhaps our equivalent today might be: 'Isn't God extraordinary?!'

In our culture many are all too ready to bring God down to our level and limit him to our own understanding. In contrast, isn't Mary's song refreshing reading? How much do we understand God's awesomeness rather than reducing him to fit our limitations?

There are three aspects of the character of God in Mary's song that I am particularly struck by: God's might, God's holiness and God's mercy. Why does Mary pick out these three in response to the news that she is going to bear the

Messiah? She is completely aware of God's lordship and her insignificance. God's amazing promise of sending his Son in human form, the very opposite of being magnified, brings out in Mary the longing to magnify him in response.

First, what does Mary sing about God's might? There are similarities between Mary's words and Hannah's song in the Old Testament. When Hannah knew that God had answered her prayer by blessing her with a son, Samuel, she responded: *'My heart rejoices in the LORD ... There is no one holy like the LORD ... those who were hungry are hungry no more ... The LORD sends poverty and wealth: he humbles and he exalts, He raises the poor from the dust ... and makes them inherit a throne of honour.'*[2] Mary also sings of a God who turns upside down human attitudes and order in society. He is able to transform the circumstances of princes and paupers, the poor and the powerful.

Secondly, what does Mary sing about God's holiness? Gabriel had told Mary that the child she is carrying *'will be called holy'*,[3] being the Son of the Most High, and she declares God's holiness, knowing her child to be his Son. She is acutely aware, like Isaiah,[4] that although she is unworthy, God is deeming to use her. How much do we fear our holy God for the right reason? This is not a fear as we might dread threats or violence, but are we aware of our own utter unworthiness in the light of God's absolute purity, goodness and holiness? Perhaps we need to recall that we are only worthy to come into God's presence because of Jesus' self-sacrifice for us.

Finally, what does Mary sing about God's mercy? We call Jesus our Saviour because of his death on the cross for us. Mary, in contrast, is calling God her Saviour because she knows she, amazingly, has been chosen and honoured; her son will be the Messiah. Mary may be a totally insignificant woman, but she has found favour with God and that means everything to her, as we looked at yesterday.

She also proclaims: *'He has filled the hungry with good things'*. There are many incidences in the Old Testament where God mercifully fed the hungry that Mary might have been familiar with. In later years she would hear that one of her son's miracles enabled 5,000 men to be fed with five loaves and two fish.[5]

How much do we take time to reflect on God's mercy – his undeserved patience and kindness – towards us? Do we readily glorify God simply for who he is? Do we then remember all that he has achieved in the past, both in the Lord Jesus and in our own lives? Do we come before him in humility? Or are we so taken up with our own agendas that we rush into requesting his intervention to help us?

Many people prominently display a photo of a loved one, smiling and relaxed. This reminds them of what's important in their life, giving them perspective. In the same way we should try, in our minds, to keep the Lord's face always before us and to fix our eyes on his eternal character. We can choose to look up and magnify the Lord, trusting in his might, keeping in mind his holiness and asking for his mercy, whatever we are facing today.

[1]   Psalm 34:3
[2]   1 Samuel 2:1–10
[3]   Luke 1:35 footnote
[4]   Isaiah 6:1–5
[5]   Mark 6:38–44
[6]   Genesis 12:2–3
[7]   Luke 1:37

Song: 'Tell out my soul' by Timothy Dudley-Smith

Name to ponder: **'The Holy One of Israel, your Saviour'** (Isaiah 43:3)

'A legend of our time'

The birth of John the Baptist

When it was time for Elizabeth to have her baby, she gave birth to a son. Her neighbours and relatives heard that the Lord had shown her great mercy, and they shared her joy.

On the eighth day they came to circumcise the child, and they were going to name him after his father Zechariah, but his mother spoke up and said, 'No! He is to be called John.'

They said to her, 'There is no one among your relatives who has that name.'

Then they made signs to his father, to find out what he would like to name the child. He asked for a writing tablet, and to everyone's astonishment he wrote, 'His name is John.' Immediately his mouth was opened and his tongue set free, and he began to speak, praising God. All the neighbours were filled with awe, and throughout the hill country of Judea people were talking about all these things. Everyone who heard this wondered about it, asking, 'What then is this child going to be?' For the Lord's hand was with him.

LUKE 1:57–66

Some people love to play games at Christmas; others will do all they can to avoid them! One of the most popular games used to be 'Charades', where groups of people guessed a book or film, for example, from clues communicated entirely through gestures and hand signals.

Zechariah would have been as eager to talk about his visit from Gabriel as Elizabeth would have been to try and comprehend what had occurred during his time away in Jerusalem on temple duty. Over the next nine months, five of which Elizabeth spent in seclusion, there would have been plenty of time to ponder. Perhaps with the help of a writing slate, lots of gesticulation or drawing in the ground, Zechariah was able to communicate something of his encounter.

And then, in the days that followed, Elizabeth maybe started to feel nauseous and even more tired than normal for her age – until it was obvious that she was, indeed, expecting a child. She certainly acknowledged the Lord's hand in granting her this special pregnancy and taking away her perceived public shame.[1]

Two days ago, we looked at what an encouragement Mary and Elizabeth might have been to each other as they pondered over the privileges with which they had both been blessed. Mary stays with Elizabeth for about three months.[2] Now the time has come for Elizabeth to give birth – to a boy, as she and Zechariah know she would. Her neighbours and relatives are delighted for her and clearly come out in force to show their support to this godly couple.

Eight days later, on the prescribed day for circumcision and official naming, and to everyone's astonishment, Zechariah communicates on a slate that the baby's name is to be John, just as Elizabeth has already told them. The instant he writes the name down, his speech returns and he immediately starts to praise God.

In all those months of silence, Zechariah has had plenty of time to consider Gabriel's visit, and when his tongue is finally loosened, he is full of praise! I wonder whether he meditated on this particular prophecy about the coming of the Messiah: *'the mute tongue [will] shout for joy'*.[3] What an astounding witness his joyous speech must be! How the neighbours must be astonished at all that is going on in this household! The entire area will have been talking about it for months, wondering what it all means and what will become of this miracle child. The forerunner of the Messiah has now been born, like a snowdrop pushing through the snow as a sign that spring is finally coming.

So, what exactly will this child grow up to be, since 'the Lord's hand' is obviously on him? Here are a few thoughts gleaned from the Old Testament prophecies and New Testament writings about his adult years as John 'the Baptist'.

In the last book of the Old Testament, the prophet Malachi foretells that God will send a messenger as the forerunner of the Messiah.[4] Indeed, Jesus himself, during his own ministry, states that John is the new Elijah.[5] Then Mark's gospel describes John wearing animal clothing and eating locusts and honey, just like Elijah, arguably the greatest Old Testament prophet of them all.[6] I love the way different parts of the Bible link together like this.

God's planning for this purpose is so perfect that it begins to come into effect over thirty years previously. Since a rabbi's ministry begins around the age of thirty, John's conception occurs six months before that of Jesus so that John can prepare people's hearts in the months before Jesus starts his own ministry. And John begins his ministry out in the wilderness, just as Jesus will do. John's ministry is only short, ending abruptly when he is imprisoned by Herod the King,[7] and later beheaded at the whim of Herod's wife.[8] Yet it is a highly significant ministry. People come in droves from the surrounding countryside to hear him talk of repentance and forgiveness of sin, and to be baptised as an outward sign of their change of heart.[9] John is the one to baptise Jesus himself, and when Jesus comes up out of the water, a voice comes from heaven confirming that he is, indeed, the Son of God.[10]

Gabriel has told Zechariah that John will be filled with the Holy Spirit from birth[11] and John's privileged status in God's plans is confirmed by Jesus' own words: *'I tell you, among those born of woman there has not risen anyone greater than John the Baptist.'*[12] Yet, John's attitude is always to point away from himself towards Jesus: *'You yourselves can testify that I said, "I am not the Messiah but am sent ahead of him." The bride belongs to the bridegroom. The friend who attends the bridegroom waits and listens for him, and is full of joy when he hears the bridegroom's voice. That joy is mine, and it is now complete. He must become greater; I must become less.'*[13] This rejoicing greatly at the bridegroom's voice reminds me of John leaping in the womb when the pregnant Mary arrives at Elizabeth's house!

On another occasion, John again points others to Jesus with these words, describing Jesus' mission in a nutshell: *'Look, the Lamb of God who takes away the sin of the world.'*[14] What a powerful summary of why Jesus comes. It is followed immediately by John stating that though he baptises with water, Jesus will baptise with the Holy Spirit, because Jesus is the Son of God.[15]

May we be people who, like John the Baptist, point others to our Saviour and prepare the way for the Lord to speak to them. May we not seek to gain favour for ourselves but want Jesus to be the centre of attention.

1   Luke 1:25
2   Luke 1: 36
3   Isaiah 35:6
4   Malachi 3:1
5   Matthew 11:13–14
6   Mark 1:6; see also 2 Kings 1:8
7   Luke 3:19–20
8   Matthew 14:6–10
9   Luke 3:3
10 Matthew 3:17
11 Luke 1:15
12 Matthew 11:11
13 John 3:28–30
14 John 1:29
15 John 1:33–34

Song: 'On Jordan's bank' by Charles Coffin (tr. J. Chandler)

Name to ponder: **'The Lord who sanctifies'** (Leviticus 20:8)

18 DECEMBER

'No time like the present'

Joseph

This is how the birth of Jesus the Messiah came about: his mother Mary was pledged to be married to Joseph, but before they came together, she was found to be pregnant through the Holy Spirit. Because Joseph her husband was faithful to the law, and yet did not want to expose her to public disgrace, he had in mind to divorce her quietly.

But after he had considered this, an angel of the Lord appeared to him in a dream and said, 'Joseph son of David, do not be afraid to take Mary home as your wife, because what is conceived in her is from the Holy Spirit. She will give birth to a son, and you are to give him the name Jesus, because he will save his people from their sins.'

MATTHEW 1:18–21

A television series about Queen Victoria reminded me of the very supportive role Albert, her husband, performed. I've also seen similar in my own era with Queen Elizabeth II, whose husband, Prince Philip, was her quiet, totally committed supporter. In today's reading from Matthew's gospel, we can see once more how extraordinarily perfect God's planning is – here in respect of Mary and Joseph's relationship.

Joseph, a carpenter, is engaged ('pledged to be married') to Mary and they both live in Nazareth. Joseph, in that culture, is therefore legally bound to Mary and so, as we considered four days ago, he already has a deep commitment to and responsibility for her. This timing is paramount. When Joseph learns of Mary's pregnancy, he is, of course, deeply disturbed, knowing that he hasn't had sexual relations with her and assuming someone else has. Having considered the situation carefully, he resolves to break off the engagement ('divorce'), but the fact that he intends to do this 'quietly' says much about his honourable character. However, an angel tells him to act otherwise, stating that Mary has conceived God's Son by the Holy Spirit's power and that Joseph should go ahead with the marriage. The angel addresses Joseph as being of the line of David, thus reminding him of the prophecy that the Messiah will be of the royal line. God is therefore inviting Joseph to trust in his promises and purposes, and to swallow his own pride. What is Joseph's reaction? He is obedient, immediately and without further questioning. What an amazing example of trusting and obeying.

The manner in which news is conveyed can in itself communicate a great deal about the message. My guess is that Mary is in some ways radiant about Gabriel's news; she has no reason to be ashamed, anguished or apologetic. Maybe this unnerves Joseph immensely, and, of course, this is a unique situation. It's not surprising he is considerably distressed.

What a tremendous relief it must be for Mary that an angel also visits Joseph in a dream to tell him what she already knows: that she has conceived by the power of the Holy Spirit. We're not told that Joseph is able to share his angst with anyone. We also are in the dark about how his family or friends react. What a man of strength to be willing to stand up in the community to protect Mary and take her as his wife, in obedience to the divine instruction.

Once he does marry her, we are specifically told that Joseph does not have sexual relations with Mary until after Jesus is born.[1] Consummating the marriage would be within his rights, having formally married Mary, but he chooses to abstain. In a culture of honour and shame, Joseph knows people will wrongly presume the baby is his and that he has pre-empted the wedding night. But, like Jesus is also to do in due course, Joseph bears the shame that isn't his. What a gracious and honourable way to act! God chooses Joseph just as much as he has chosen Mary, although the limelight falls so much less on him. Joseph's job is on the sidelines, but his support and provision for Mary are of paramount importance.

One of the consequences of Joseph's obedience is that he is privileged to witness the most significant event in history, the most important birth ever. It is he who legally names the child with the name given by the angel. By doing this, Joseph clearly asserts that he is committed to Jesus' care.

God's plans are not what Joseph would have had in mind, but he graciously accepts them and plays his part to the full. He supports Mary (who in that society would be an outcast for carrying an apparently illegitimate baby) and will bring up Jesus during his childhood. As a Jewish father, it will be his responsibility to raise Jesus with an understanding of the Jewish ways, and through the year to teach him festivals and history from the Torah. Can you imagine Jesus sitting on Joseph's lap, or later perhaps sitting with him in the synagogue, hearing passages from Old Testament prophets that referred to him? I wonder too how Joseph feels hearing those prophecies referring to the future suffering of the boy next to him.[2]

Joseph isn't talked about in the gospels after Jesus' temple visit aged twelve, although Matthew later mentions the children Joseph has with Mary: four sons – James, Joseph,

Simon and Judas – and at least three unnamed daughters.[3] He is presumably not alive by the time of Jesus' crucifixion, when Mary is entrusted by Jesus to 'the disciple whom he loved'.[4]

Could we find in Joseph's initial uncertainty some help and encouragement when we might feel unsure about God's ways and what he might be asking us to do? Are we prepared to listen to God and follow his guidance, even when it's different to our plans or what we had hoped for? Will we trust and obey? And if we are called to play a supporting role, whatever that is – whether in our families, in our workplace or in our communities – are we willing to do that to the best of our ability? I'm so grateful for examples like this man Joseph.

[1]   Matthew 1:25
[2]   See, for example, Isaiah 53:3–10
[3]   Matthew 13:55–56
[4]   John 19:26

Song: 'I am a Carpenter' by Cher and Gene Klosner

Name to ponder: **'El Roi – The God who sees'** (Genesis 16:13)

19 DECEMBER

'A step at a time'

Bethlehem and the census

In those days Caesar Augustus issued a decree that a census should be taken of the entire Roman world. This was the first census that took place while Quirinius was governor of Syria. And everyone went to their own town to register.

So Joseph also went up from the town of Nazareth in Galilee to Judea, to Bethlehem the town of David, because he belonged to the house and line of David. He went there to register with Mary, who was pledged to be married to him and was expecting a child.

LUKE 2:1–5

Today's reading brings together the culture and history of two nations for the birth of God's Son. Again, God's perfect timing fills me with awe and wonder. The Roman emperor, Augustus – lord of one of history's greatest empires – issues his command for a census throughout the Roman-controlled world. This in turn leads to Joseph, a carpenter in the province of Judea, heading with his pregnant fiancée back to his ancestral hometown of Bethlehem – a town richly associated with Israel's national heritage as the birthplace of their greatest king, David, from whose line Joseph comes.

In ancient Palestine, there were actually two places called Bethlehem, much as we have places of the same name in the UK – like Newcastle-upon-Tyne or Newcastle-under-Lyme. The important Bethlehem, mentioned in our reading, is Bethlehem Ephrathah and appears a number of times in the Old Testament.

In Genesis, Isaac's wife Rachel is buried on the way to Bethlehem: *'So Rachel died and was buried on the way to Ephrath (that is, Bethlehem).'*[1] This town therefore has an association with Abraham's own family.

In the book of Ruth, we read of Elimelech and his wife Naomi, who leave Bethlehem during a famine and go to Moab.[2] When Naomi's husband and both her sons die there, she returns with her daughter-in-law Ruth to Bethlehem,[3] where Ruth gleans in a field belonging to Naomi's kinsman, Boaz.[4] Boaz marries Ruth, announcing that her former husband's name will not disappear from Bethlehem's town records.[5] The witnesses to the wedding give a remarkable blessing to Boaz: *'May the Lord make the woman who is coming into your home like Rachel and Leah, who together built up the house of Israel. May you have standing in Ephrathah and be famous in Bethlehem. Through the offspring the Lord gives you by this young woman, may your family be like that of Perez, whom Tamar bore to Judah.'*[6] The book of Ruth ends, as quoted in the genealogy presented at the start of Matthew's gospel,[7] with the family line from Judah's son, Perez, to Jesse, the father of David.[8]

In 1 Samuel, God sends Samuel to Bethlehem to anoint one of Jesse's sons as king to replace Saul.[9] Soon after we read: *'David went back and forth from Saul to tend his father's sheep at Bethlehem.'*[10] Then the writer of 2 Chronicles records that Solomon's son Rehoboam, having been rejected by most of the tribes of Israel, fortified towns in Judah; the list begins with Bethlehem.[11]

Micah, living in the eight century BC – in a passage often read in Christmas services – prophesies the importance of Bethlehem as the place from which a great king will come: *'But you, Bethlehem Ephrathah, though you are small among the clans of Judah, out of you will come for me one who will be ruler over Israel, whose origins are from of old, from ancient times.'*[12] It is this prophecy that leads the chief priests and teachers of the law to tell Herod, disconcerted by the visit of the Magi, that he should look to Bethlehem to find the one born as king of the Jews.[13]

In Ezra, we read among the list of the exiles returning from Babylon to Jerusalem (in 538 BC) that there were 123 men from Bethlehem,[14] along with Zerubbabel, among whose descendants would be Jesus' father, Joseph.

This is a brief recap of Bethlehem's importance in the Old Testament, but the last reference serves as a reminder of the significance of keeping records. For the Israelites, records show where people belonged. Joseph returns to Bethlehem from Nazareth because that is where the proof of his identity exists. Although the Emperor Augustus is primarily concerned with his tax revenues when ordering the census, the fact it forces everyone to return to their hometowns means Micah's prophecy from over 700 years earlier can be fulfilled.

For Joseph to meet the requirement of the census, the journey to Bethlehem has to be taken; there were no postal electoral forms then! So he sets out with the betrothed, heavily pregnant Mary to travel around eighty miles via the valley of the River Jordan, over some rough and hilly terrain. People in that culture were used to these sorts of journey, for example to celebrate the Passover in Jerusalem (and we have already seen Mary visiting her cousin Elizabeth earlier with a similar journey time). But this trip involves some days and nights of serious discomfort for

Mary near to full term. Perhaps others, even wider family members, are on the same route to obey the summons of the census, but this isn't an easy journey for Mary – with no rest in the final stage of her pregnancy and without the comfort of a home birth.

Have we grasped the wonder of God's sovereignty over the mighty emperor of Rome? Augustus rules from Spain to Syria, from Morocco to Egypt. His empire's boundaries are the Atlantic Ocean to the west, the Sahara Desert to the south, the Rhine and Danube Rivers to the north, and various Middle Eastern kingdoms to the east. Yet a decision taken by this one man leads to the fulfilment of a centuries-old prophecy in a little town in Judea through the birth of Jesus. This same Jesus would in time create a worldwide following, through his death and resurrection. When he returns at his second coming, every knee will bow at *his* name, before whom the mighty Augustus will pale into insignificance. Yet first, as God so often does, he turns the expected upside down. A carpenter (albeit of an ancient royal line) must take his pregnant fiancée to a little town in a backwater of the Roman Empire. That is the place where her son must be born.

1   Genesis 35:19
2   Ruth 1:1
3   Ruth 1:19
4   Ruth 2:3
5   Ruth 4:10
6   Ruth 4:11–12
7   Matthew 1:3–6
8   Ruth 4:18–22
9   1 Samuel 16:1
10   1 Samuel 17:15
11   2 Chronicles 11:5–6

12   Micah 5:2
13   Matthew 2:1–6
14   Ezra 2:1–2, 21

🎧   Song: 'O little town of Bethlehem' by Phillips Brooks

🙏   Name to ponder: **'The God who knows'** (1 Samuel 2:3)

20 DECEMBER

'Behind the times'

Background to Luke 2

This is what the Lord says: 'You say about this place, "It is a desolate waste, without people or animals." Yet in the towns of Judah and the streets of Jerusalem that are deserted, inhabited by neither people nor animals, there will be heard once more the sounds of joy and gladness, the voices of bride and bridegroom, and the voices of those who bring thank offerings to the house of the Lord, saying,

"Give thanks to the Lord Almighty,
    for the Lord is good;
    his love endures forever."

'For I will restore the fortunes of the land as they were before,' says the Lord.
    This is what the Lord Almighty says: 'In this place, desolate and without people or animals – in all its towns there will again be pastures for shepherds to rest their flocks. In the towns of the hill country, of the western foothills and of the Negev, in the territory of Benjamin, in the villages around Jerusalem and in the towns of Judah, flocks will again pass under the hand of the one who counts them,' says the Lord.

'The days are coming,' declares the Lord,
'when I will fulfil the good promise I made to
the people of Israel and Judah.

"In those days and at that time
    I will make a righteous Branch sprout from
    David's line;
    he will do what is just and right in the land.

In those days Judah will be saved
    and Jerusalem will live in safety.
This is the name by which it will be called:
    The Lord Our Righteous Saviour.'"

JEREMIAH 33:10–16

And there were shepherds living out in the
fields near by, keeping watch over their flock at
night.

LUKE 2:8

The glorious readings at carol services can become perhaps
so familiar that, unless some understanding of the backstory
is also presented, the culmination of all the extraordinary
fulfilments of Old Testament prophecies is missed.

A few days ago, we read about Daniel pondering
Jeremiah's God-given prophecy that the exile of the Jews to
Babylon would last for seventy years before God intervened
to enable the Jews to return to the land that he had promised
them. This happened just as the angel Gabriel explained to
him.

Our reading today also comes from Jeremiah, who is
prophesying at a time when the land of Judah is 'desolate'
and ruined from the terrible ravages of war – examples of
which we've seen all too often in the media. In our UK lock-

downs of 2020 and 2021, there was an eerie silence stemming from an absence of traffic, playground noise and laughter in the streets. Back then in Judah the misery was much, much worse, with the devastating silence of an abandoned and broken land.

When Jeremiah speaks into this situation with his prophecies, it seems inconceivable that they will come true. Will God really bring his people back from their exile to Babylon and restore the land? Will there really again be the everyday sounds of normal life? Yet we read that the exiles do return to the land promised to Abraham's descendants – first by permission of Cyrus king of Persia, and led by Zerubbabel;[1] and secondly, by permission of another king, Artaxerxes, with one group under Ezra[2] and a later group under Nehemiah.[3] Some normality of life for Judah can resume once more.

By the time Luke's gospel account begins, Judea is under occupation by the Romans, but life is largely able to continue freely. In Luke's simple sentence, we have a fabulous understatement that there *are* shepherds abiding in the fields! This is a deliberate detail to highlight that God continues to keep his promises. Centuries before he had brought the people back to Judah, and now he is indeed about to bring someone from the line of David. He will choose to announce this news to shepherds (of all people!) – to those pasturing their flocks, as Jeremiah foretold: 'in the villages around Jerusalem and in the towns of Judah'.

The world depicted in Jeremiah's prophecy reminds me of C S. Lewis' book *The Lion, the Witch and the Wardrobe*, where the land of Narnia, covered in snow and trapped in winter, starts to show signs of spring coming. The snow begins to melt, which greatly alarms the White Witch and her supporters, as it signifies the end of her bleak reign. And with spring comes new life and goodness.

As Luke writes his gospel account of Judea, God has already fulfilled Jeremiah's extraordinary prophecies: there are 'the sounds of joy and gladness' as the local community delights at the birth of John; 'the voices of bride and bridegroom' with Joseph and Mary's engagement – an event presumably full of celebration; and 'the voices of those who bring thank offerings to the house of the LORD' as Zechariah serves as a priest in the temple in Jerusalem.

Perhaps before we move on to focus our thoughts on the events of that first Christmas, it would be good to pause to remember again that other important theme of Advent: that one day the Lord Jesus will return in glory. Prophecies on that climactic event have also been given to us in the Scriptures.[4] Are we wholeheartedly trusting in Jesus' promised return and preparing for that Day?

Over the next few days, we will be staying with Luke's gospel account, since for him this is only the start. The voices of gladness may already be echoing around the hills of Judah at the birth of John, but the rejoicing to come will eclipse that as an announcement is made that God is sending his Son to bring salvation to the world.

[1]   Ezra 1:1–3; 2:1–2

[2]   Ezra 7:1–7

[3]   Nehemiah 2:1–11

[4]   See, for example, Zechariah 9:14; Isaiah 59:15–20; 60:1–3, 19–20; 62:11–12; Matthew 24:30

Song: 'From the breaking of the dawn' by Stuart Townend and Keith Getty

Name to ponder: **'Wonderful Counsellor'** (Isaiah 9:6)

'Biding their time'

The shepherds

> And there were shepherds living out in the fields near by, keeping watch over their flocks at night. An angel of the Lord appeared to them, and the glory of the Lord shone around them, and they were terrified. But the angel said to them, 'Do not be afraid. I bring you good news that will cause great joy for all the people.'
>
> LUKE 2:8–10

Our reading today takes us back to the fields around Bethlehem, where a group of shepherds are caring for their flock at night, just as David had in those very same fields hundreds of years previously. Before we look at this extraordinary news of the Messiah's birth, let's pause today to consider who the recipients of the message are and what accompanies the announcement.

Rural Berkshire, where we lived for a number of years, has few streetlights and is therefore pitch black at night. Out in the countryside can initially be a confusing and disorientating place to be, but then you become used to it. As the shepherds were accustomed to darkness, the sudden appearance of an angel and the blazing light of heaven that shone down on the surrounding fields must have been incredibly alarming. Unsurprisingly, these tough guys are terrified, but are immediately reassured by the angel.

This group of surely hardened men were used to warding off wild animals and sleeping rough under the night sky. What a privilege to be the first people on earth, ever, to hear that the Messiah has been born! How wonderful and awe-inspiring that this news is revealed to them, shepherds – not to the High Priest or one of his team in the temple over in the city of Jerusalem, or to King Herod and his entourage, or even to the probably high-ranking and educated Magi who will come to visit Bethlehem later.

Given what we have been reading these past few days about God's ways, that shouldn't surprise us! What reassurance that God's salvation is for *all* people, especially the 'outcasts' of this world. Yet there is a challenge too: God turns upside down our customary attitudes and prejudices, showing his concern for those in whom we might arrogantly assume he will not be interested. He chooses shepherds, ordinary men, considered by most people then as religiously unclean! As the angel says, how better to illustrate that this great news is for 'all the people'. Doesn't this give us hope? We, too, are totally unworthy, but through the grace of our Lord Jesus, we can be made clean, spotless and acceptable to our holy God![1]

No priest could enter the inner sections of the temple without the most rigorous rituals of purification and unless wearing exactly the right ceremonial clothes.[2] This again highlights how astounding it is that the local shepherds, for whom hygiene would not be a top priority to say the least, are privileged to witness this heavenly appearance. But the prophet Isaiah had said centuries before: '*The Lord says …* "*Therefore once more I will astound these people with wonder upon wonder.*"'[3]

We are told that 'the glory of the Lord shone around

them,' so these shepherds are given a glimpse into heaven! We don't have anything particular in modern life to equate with this word 'glory', and a definition of what it exactly means is not perhaps straightforward. I think it is the manifestation of the highest possible magnificence of the presence of God. Is it best encapsulated by David's prayer in 2 Chronicles: *'Yours, LORD, is the greatness and the power and the glory and the majesty and the splendour, for everything in heaven and on earth is yours.'*[4]

Let's look at two instances from Exodus that also mention the 'glory of the Lord'. When Moses goes up a mountain to meet with God, it says that *'the glory of the LORD settled on Mount Sinai'* and this is described as a cloud covering the mountain for six days; to the Israelites encamped in the plain, this glory looks like a consuming fire upon the mountain top.[5] Later in Exodus, God gives instructions to Moses as to how he wants the tabernacle to be assembled, since he is going to come down and dwell among his people. We are told that once the tabernacle has been constructed, *'the glory of the LORD filled the tabernacle'*, barring even Moses from entering it.[6] Might the appearance of the angel to the shepherds, when 'the glory of the Lord shone around them', be something similar? No wonder that it is an absolutely terrifying sight!

The writer to the Hebrews states that Jesus *'is the radiance of God's glory'*,[7] and Jesus himself says that he is *'the light of the world'*;[8] it's no wonder that his birth is signalled by such extraordinary light!

The verses from today's reading challenge me to ask myself again whether my view of God is often far too small. Perhaps you could spend time imagining what this experience must have been like for those shepherds, who were quietly looking after their sheep in the fields one night long ago and whose lives could never be the same again? Yet, we have the privilege of being able to read the book of Revelation, where we are given a glimpse into heaven's continuous praise of God. There: *'the voice of many angels, numbering thousands upon thousands, and ten thousand times ten thousand'* continuously worship God, seated on his throne.[9]

One final thought for today: Jesus calls himself the *'good shepherd'*[10], and in Isaiah there is a prediction concerning how this Messiah will treat his people: *'He tends his flock like a shepherd; he gathers the lambs in his arms and carries them close to his heart; he gently leads those that have young.'*[11] It therefore seems highly appropriate to me that it is a group of shepherds who first hear the news that a Saviour has been born this night. Shepherds had a key role in choosing the unblemished lambs to be offered in the temple as sacrifices; now some of them hear about the birth of God's own Son, who one day will be the perfect sacrifice for the sin of the world, the Lamb of God.

[1] Isaiah 64:6; 1 John 1:7
[2] Exodus 28
[3] Isaiah 29:13–14
[4] 1 Chronicles 29:11
[5] Exodus 24:15–17
[6] Exodus 40:34–35
[7] Hebrews 1:3
[8] John 8:12
[9] Revelation 5:11
[10] John 10:11
[11] Isaiah 40:11

'While shepherds watched their flocks' by Nahum Tate

Name to ponder: **'The Lamb of God'** (John 1:29)

'The time has come'

The angels' announcement

And there were shepherds living out in the fields near by, keeping watch over their flocks at night. An angel of the Lord appeared to them, and the glory of the Lord shone around them, and they were terrified. But the angel said to them, 'Do not be afraid. I bring you good news that will cause great joy for all the people. Today in the town of David a Saviour has been born to you; he is the Messiah, the Lord. This will be a sign to you: you will find a baby wrapped in cloths and lying in a manger.'

Suddenly a great company of the heavenly host appeared with the angel, praising God and saying,

'Glory to God in the highest heaven,
and on earth peace to those on whom his
favour rests.'

LUKE 2:8–14

In recent years, reality TV programmes such as *Britain's Got Talent* have started the trend of building suspense for a minute or so at the end of each episode. Contestants have to stand in the spotlight before it is revealed who is going through to the next round and who is out of the competition.

There is dramatic music, perhaps a countdown and camera shots of anxious faces and trembling lips before the announcement is made. In the final show, the tension is heightened all the more and the result is announced to the accompaniment of gasps, shocked faces, tears of disbelief, hugs, confetti cascading down and cameras focusing in on the successful winners.

The moment of the Messiah's arrival couldn't have been more different. After hundreds of years waiting, hopes of a Messiah have been well and truly dashed for all but a faithful few. But now heaven simply can't wait to make its glorious announcement; utter joy erupts with triumphant exhilaration. The angels burst out of the dark skies, turning on all the spotlights at once, as it were, in a dazzling, magnificent performance!

We can become so familiar with hearing the angel's statement read out in Christmas carol services that we miss its awesome significance: 'Today in the town of David a Saviour has been born to you; he is the Messiah, the Lord.'

This is an astonishing, earth-shattering announcement of an event that previously has only been communicated in private to Mary, Joseph and Zechariah. The city of David refers to Bethlehem, and the name 'Christ' is the Greek for the Hebrew word for 'Messiah'. There can be no misunderstanding of the message; it is crystal clear: the Messiah has been born, and born in the predicted place of Bethlehem, and this has literally just happened 'today'. The angels seem unable to suppress their overwhelming joy that at last the plan to save mankind can be revealed.

We will be looking more at the amazing truth of Jesus' incarnation over the next few days, but for today let's reflect on two things. First, the sign given by the angel to the shepherds, and secondly, the heavenly choir and their message.

If someone visits our hometown and asks us for

directions to a specific place, we might try to think of obvious landmarks to act as signs, guiding them to their destination. In the Bible, signs are visible symbols of God at work; they are reminders of his presence, power and promises. Sometimes they are miraculous in revealing God's awesome nature and his faithfulness, such as the first rainbow that appears in the sky after the flood (in which only the righteous Noah and his family survive) as a promise that God will never again destroy all life.[1] As we know from the Christmas narrative, another sign is a virgin being with child.[2] At other times signs are very down-to-earth and easy to understand, like finding a colt tied up in the street, as Jesus prepares for his triumphant entry into Jerusalem.[3]

In the angel's message, the shepherds are given a sign with which they are very familiar: a manger. This newborn baby will be found in an animal feeding trough. Though perhaps this imagery is familiar to us, it points the shepherds to a highly unusual situation: Mary will not be feeding the baby Jesus, Joseph will not be holding him and Jesus won't be strapped to either of them by a makeshift sling.

The baby will specifically be lying in the manger at the exact time that the shepherds come looking; that is how they will recognise him in a town that might well be home to other babies as well. The timing is yet again absolutely crucial as the shepherds know nothing else about Jesus' location in the village or the names of the parents. Though unexpected, the sign of the manger is vital, down-to-earth, familiar and entirely in keeping with the humility of God's Son.

Secondly, what a performance a host of heaven's angels then gives as the backing group to the first angel's message. Reflecting on the wonder of God's Son being born, they can't keep quiet their delight! At last, they can tell of God's intricate plan with tremendous excitement, their joy and amazement spilling down to earth. This is no softly sung choir; this is a jolt-them-out-of-their-seats-at-full-volume choir! It is a fabulous sneak preview of the continuous celebration in heaven.

What exactly is the angelic choir's message? They give glory to God – not glory to themselves, nor to anyone else, nor even to Mary. God has fulfilled his plan, which was years and years in its preparation and foretelling. This is the moment that has been awaited; now, on this day, it is finally revealed to humankind! Glory indeed to God, for his graciousness in sending his precious, only Son to earth, knowing and intending that he would die thirty or so years later to bring us back to God. Jesus will open up the way for us to enjoy once more the full relationship for which God created us.

It is so easy to take away from God the praise that is due to him. Mary might have been chosen as the only woman ever to have this privilege, but it wasn't her glory to take. The glory for this awesome incarnate birth belongs to God! When Jesus comes again, we all, believers or not, will worship him on bended knee, alongside shepherds and kings. Wouldn't it be wonderful if we were able to cultivate an attitude that automatically gives God the glory for who he is, what he has done, and what he continues to do in our lives and in our world?

1   Genesis 9:12–15
2   Isaiah 7:14
3   Mark 11:4–6; see also Zechariah 9:9

Song: 'Glory to God in the highest, and peace on earth, good-will toward men' from Handel's *Messiah*

Name to ponder: **'Christ the Lord'** (Luke 2:11)

'Having the time of their lives'

The shepherds and Mary

While they were there, the time came for the baby to be born, and she gave birth to her firstborn, a son. She wrapped him in cloths and placed him in a manger, because there was no guest room available for them …

When the angels had left them and gone into heaven, the shepherds said to one another, 'Let's go to Bethlehem and see this thing that has happened, which the Lord has told us about.'

So they hurried off and found Mary and Joseph, and the baby, who was lying in the manger. When they had seen him, they spread the word concerning what had been told them about this child, and all who heard it were amazed at what the shepherds said to them. But Mary treasured up all these things and pondered them in her heart. The shepherds returned, glorifying and praising God for all the things they had heard and seen, which were just as they had been told.

LUKE 2:6–7, 15–20

With typical understatement, in just two sentences, Luke writes that on arriving at Bethlehem after a journey of a number of days, Mary goes into labour and gives birth to Jesus. That there isn't a decent place for them to stay is almost brushed over as of no consequence, with every available place presumably occupied because of the census.

In that society, it would be unthinkable for family not to provide for one of their own – whatever disgrace to the family honour is caused by the shame of an unmarried woman's pregnancy. But with so many relatives arriving day after day, it seems that the only available floor space that can be offered to Mary is with the animals. At that time, animals would often be housed near the family living area, and kept under the same roof for their safety as well as the warmth they provided at night. There simply wasn't anywhere else for Jesus to be laid but in the animal's food trough. Mary and Joseph will have been totally oblivious to the fact that that is the exact place God intends his newborn Son to be laid; it is an absolutely essential sign for the visitors already hastening to meet this baby.

We will think about the extraordinary fact of the birth of God's Son over the coming days, but first let's return our focus to the shepherds. Specifically, let's look at their reactions to what they have heard and then see. We will also reflect on Mary's reactions to these events, as she hears their remarkable story.

Whenever our government bestows honours in the name of our monarch, generally the recipients are informed several weeks in advance. They are required to keep the news private until the embargo is lifted and the list published. Some might then react by going public and posting their honour on social media, while others will want to remain private. The shepherds' response to the honour of hearing about the birth of the Messiah is to tell anyone and everyone; in contrast, Mary's reaction to both their arrival and then their news is to ponder and treasure these matters in her heart.

Immediately the angel leaves the shepherds, they hurry off to Bethlehem without delay – not from mere curiosity but because they are utterly convinced by the angel's message. Others might consider themselves unworthy to visit the newborn Messiah, but the shepherds know that they have specifically been invited! (The pronoun 'you' is used by the angel with great emphasis four times in verses 10–12!)

Yet again, the words that God's newborn Son will be laid in a manger can become so familiar to us (and are sometimes read at carol services without an iota of astonishment). No royal baby would be laid in an animal feeding trough ... But how typical of God, in his extraordinary humility and kindness, to lay his Son in a manger with which these shepherds are familiar. They could relate to the humble circumstances in which Jesus was born as they drew near to visit him in a lowly village home.

The shepherds have nothing to bring as gifts; they come just as they are. Yet their enthusiasm for and acceptance of the truth they've been told is evident as they relate everything. Once the shepherds have seen the baby lying in a manger, their reaction is to go home praising and glorifying God, and telling others about what has happened. The shepherds, therefore, are the very first evangelists to the good news of Jesus! Are we still thrilled by the Christmas story and what it stands for?

The shepherds react to their unexpected visit from the angels in the fields and to meeting the Messiah themselves with exuberant praise and witness. What is Mary's reaction to her unexpected visitors? 'Mary treasured up all these things and pondered them in her heart.'

When Jesus is born in a stable or the part of a house used to keep animals, there are no angels, no trumpet blasts and no royal announcement. No voice from on high says to Jesus: 'You are my Son, whom I love' (as was to come publicly thirty or so years later, when Jesus is baptised in the River Jordan at the start of his ministry).[1] Nor are the shepherds the visitors Mary might expect (if she is expecting any at all) – there are certainly no High Priest, scribes nor Pharisees flocking at the door begging to glimpse the Messiah.

Yet the shepherds' arrival must be an extraordinary reassurance to Mary, who is far from home, has just endured childbirth and is presumably exhausted. Apart from Elizabeth's affirmation, we assume there has been silence from heaven in the nine months since both Mary and Joseph were visited by an angel. But now these men out in the field have heard the news by divine announcement – how else could they have possibly known it? Then they have immediately come with such enthusiasm to rejoice and celebrate with Mary and Joseph. No wonder she locks these precious details away in her heart and returns to them again and again in her mind.

Perhaps some of us are more like Mary than the shepherds? Maybe we do not have the temperament that bursts out exuberantly with joy, causing us to tell everyone about our faith. But do we treasure these truths in our hearts and enjoy meditating on the wonder of the Christmas narrative? There is room for both reactions and everything in between! However we react, we can wonder at God's wonderful timing and planning, which Luke deliberately draws attention to in today's reading with the phrase '*as they had been told*'. Those words will be used twice more in his gospel account of the end of Jesus' life – at his triumphal entry and then again on the night before he died.[2] Everything is in God's plan.

[1] Mark 1:11
[2] Luke 19:32; 22:13

Song: 'Manger throne' by Phil Wickham

Name to ponder: **'Beloved Son'** (Mark 1:11)

24 DECEMBER

'Time immemorial'

The pre-incarnate Jesus

In the beginning was the Word, and the Word was with God, and the Word was God. He was with God in the beginning. Through him all things were made; without him nothing was made that has been made.

JOHN 1:1–3

When John writes his gospel, he gives us the big picture in his first three verses – Jesus existed with the Father before the creation of the world and before his birth in Bethlehem!

While investigating the location of a particular landmark in a village or town, using the search engine Google Earth, I have occasionally inadvertently zoomed out onto the whole of Europe! But John is intentional in expanding our outlook, commencing with the perspective of the entire universe and the explanation that Jesus has always existed in eternity. After that he zooms in, narrating his account of Jesus' life, death and resurrection. Although our traditional dating system uses BC/AD for before Christ and in the year of the Lord, actually there was never a time before Christ.

Today we will simply be meditating on the wonderful meaning of John's first three verses by reflecting on a number of other verses that make reference to Jesus' pre-existence. We start with verses in Genesis and Isaiah, which introduce, faintly, the concept of the eternal Trinity. Then there are more verses from later in John's gospel and some from other New Testament writers. This is not an exhaustive list but I have also chosen these verses to show the importance of this theological truth and to help us approach Christmas Day with even more awe and wonder. (The emphasis in each verse is mine.)

> *In the beginning was the Word, and the Word was with God, and the Word was God.*
>
> JOHN 1:1

> *Then God said, 'Let us make mankind in* our *image, in* our *likeness.'*
>
> GENESIS 1:26

> *Who will go for* us?
>
> ISAIAH 6:8

> *Then what if you see the Son of Man ascend to where* he was before?
>
> JOHN 6:62

> *'Very truly I tell you,' Jesus answered,* 'before Abraham was born, I am!'
>
> JOHN 8:58

> *… but now I am going to him* who sent me.
>
> JOHN 16:5

> I came from the Father *and entered the world; now I am leaving the world and going back to the Father.*
>
> JOHN 16:28

And now, Father, glorify me in your presence
with the glory I had with you before the world
began.

JOHN 17:5

Father, I want those you have given me to be with
me where I am, and to see my glory, the glory
you have given me because you loved me before
the creation of the world.

JOHN 17:24

He has saved us and called us to a holy life – not
because of anything we have done but because of
his own purpose and grace. This grace was given
us in Christ Jesus before the beginning of time,
but it has now been revealed through the
appearing of our Savior, Christ Jesus.

2 TIMOTHY 1:9–10

Otherwise Christ would have had to suffer many
times since the creation of the world.

HEBREWS 9:26

That which was from the beginning, *which we*
have heard, which we have seen with our eyes,
which we have looked at and our hands have
touched – this we proclaim concerning the Word
of life. The life appeared; we have seen it and
testify to it, and we proclaim to you the eternal
life, which was with the Father and has appeared
to us.

1 JOHN 1:1–2

Do not be afraid. I am the First and the Last. *I am the Living One; I was dead, and now look, I am alive for ever and ever!*

REVELATION 1:17–18

In the beginning was the Word, and the Word was with God, and the Word was God.

JOHN 1:1

Hallelujah!

Song: 'You're the Word of God the Father' by Stuart Townend and Keith Getty

Name to ponder: **'The Alpha and the Omega'**
(Revelation 21:6)

25 DECEMBER

'At a particular point in time'

The incarnation (part 1)

In the beginning was the Word, and the Word was with God, and the Word was God. He was with God in the beginning. Through him all things were made; without him nothing was made that has been made. In him was life, and that life was the light of all mankind. The light shines in the darkness, and the darkness has not overcome it ...

The true light that gives light to everyone was coming into the world. He was in the world, and though the world was made through him, the world did not recognise him. He came to that which was his own, but his own did not receive him. Yet to all who did receive him, to those who believed in his name, he gave the right to become children of God – children born not of natural descent, nor of human decision or a husband's will, but born of God.

The Word became flesh and made his dwelling among us. We have seen his glory, the glory of the one and only Son, who came from the Father, full of grace and truth.

JOHN 1:1–5, 9–14 (my emphasis)

101

'Christ is Risen!' is a common greeting on Easter Sunday morning, and perhaps we could greet fellow believers with 'Christ is born!' on this very special day. We meet together to celebrate the remembrance of such a momentous historical event!

Our reading for Christmas Day gives us an opportunity to stand back and marvel again at the extraordinary Christian claim that God became human: the mystery of the incarnation. We have already looked at the first three verses of this reading but we will spend the next two days reflecting on the last verse above: the unfathomable claim and mystery that Jesus Christ is both fully human and fully God.

Is it of any consequence whether Jesus was 100% man and 100% God, or would 50:50 be reasonable to believe? The Romans, Judea's occupying force at that time, worshipped demi-gods such as Hercules. He was thought to be a super-human figure during his lifetime (being the son of Jupiter, the king of the gods, and of Alcmena, a woman), then becoming a god when he died. In contrast, the Christian faith teaches that Jesus, while being born a human being just as we are, is also, always fully God.

The apostle John puts the importance of Jesus' incarnation perhaps surprisingly strongly: *'This is how you can recognise the Spirit of God: every spirit that acknowledges that Jesus Christ has come in the flesh is from God, but every spirit that does not acknowledge Jesus is not from God.'*[1] In other words, for the Christian, the deity of the human Christ is non-negotiable, in contrast to how other religions view Jesus. The incarnation of Jesus is as central to our faith as the resurrection of Jesus, and through it Jesus embodies both humility and glory.

The humility of Jesus

Nick Vujicic is a Christian evangelist and motivational speaker. He was born without limbs, a syndrome affecting only a few families in the world. In his autobiography *Life without Limits* he describes the moment when he met a toddler born with the same syndrome and had a dawning realisation and excitement that he could support this boy in his future. Equipped with the knowledge of how he had dealt with the distress, rejection and hardships that he knew this boy would also experience, Nick hoped that he might be able to inspire him. Nick was in the (almost) unique position of completely understanding the boy's situation. In a far greater way, Jesus left the glory of heaven to become one of us, to immerse himself unreservedly and completely in human life on earth and experience everything that we go through.

Personally, I find it mind-blowing that the pre-existing and divine Son of God becomes almost imperceptibly microscopic in Mary's uterus. For me, it's no problem for God, the author of life, to create an embryo from just an egg – that's not the amazing point. The idea I find extraordinary to grasp is that God's Son limits himself so massively to become that human embryo, initially less than the size of this full stop. Jesus leaves his divine status behind in heaven and chooses to humble himself that much. He doesn't give up his nature, but he does give up his status; he willingly lays aside all the privileges that he has in heaven. In giving up his rights, God's Son can identify with the least of us.

As God, Jesus exists as the 'Most High'; in taking on human flesh, he becomes 'most low'. The glory of heaven is exchanged for a manger. The omnipotent architect of creation becomes an impotent baby, utterly dependent on the care of his human mother and unable to do anything whatsoever himself; he becomes completely vulnerable.

But as well as being born in humble circumstances, in a little town in a remote part of the Roman Empire, Jesus will go on to fulfil all the requirements of the law – circumcision and purification – and humbly obey Mary and Joseph. And, of course, at the end of his earthly life, Jesus will allow himself to be mocked, flogged and killed, a victim of Jewish and Roman authorities, who feel threatened by his actions and words.

The glory of Jesus

Paradoxically, it is this very characteristic of humility which enhances Jesus' glory and raises his humanity to a new status. The writer to the Hebrews tells us: *'The Son is the radiance of God's glory and the exact representation of his being.'*[2] The apostle John, in our reading for today, is in awe that he has witnessed with his own eyes the glory of God's only Son. This glory is displayed in Jesus' earthly ministry by his miracles (such as healings and power over nature), his authority to forgive sin and his ability to foretell the future. John also witnesses Jesus' crowning glory: his death, resurrection and ascension. John and the other apostles begin to understand the glory of the cross: that only someone fully human can die and be an acceptable sacrifice to God for sin – for God, being immortal in nature, cannot die. Then God raises Jesus the man from the dead, showing that he has accepted him as a perfect sacrifice for our sin.

I also find it awe-inspiring that the resurrected Jesus acquires an additional authority and status that he doesn't have before he comes to earth: he is now and forever seated at the right hand of the Father, fully God and fully human.

How incredible that Jesus, fully God and fully human, is already in heaven and that one day he will return in glory to judge the living and the dead. As we read in Acts: *'This same*

Jesus, who has been taken from you into heaven, will come back in the same way you have seen him go into heaven.'[3] As Acts goes on to explain about God the Father's judgement on the world: *'For he has set a day when he will judge the world with justice by the man he has appointed. He has given proof of this to everyone by raising him from the dead.'*[4]

I hope today's reflections have helped you be filled with awe and wonder at this extraordinary mathematical paradox: Jesus is 100% God and 100% human.

[1] 1 John 4:2–3 (my emphasis)
[2] Hebrews 1:3
[3] Acts 1:11
[4] Acts 17:31

Song: 'O magnum mysterium' by Morten Lauridsen

If opportunity allows, listen to this quietly, perhaps with just a candle in the darkness, to help you reflect on the wonder of these words. Ask God to help you feel afresh something of the magnitude of what he has done in coming to earth in human flesh.

Name to ponder: **'Word of God'** (John 1:1)

'Taking time to be with us'

The incarnation (part 2)

In the beginning was the Word, and the Word was with God, and the Word was God. He was with God in the beginning. Through him all things were made; without him nothing was made that has been made. In him was life, and that life was the light of all mankind. The light shines in the darkness, and the darkness has not overcome it...

The true light that gives light to everyone was coming into the world. He was in the world, and though the world was made through him, the world did not recognise him. He came to that which was his own, but his own did not receive him. Yet to all who did receive him, to those who believed in his name, he gave the right to become children of God – children born not of natural descent, nor of human decision or a husband's will, but born of God.

The Word became flesh and made his dwelling among us. We have seen his glory, the glory of the one and only Son, who came from the Father, full of grace and truth.

JOHN 1:1–5, 9–14

Yesterday we reflected on the paradox of both the humility and the glory of Jesus being born in human form. Today we are going to consider the paradox of the God who is utterly holy and unapproachable coming to dwell among fallen human beings. The apostle John proudly and boldly states: *'We have seen ... the one and only Son'.*

The unapproachability of God

The Old Testament, on numerous occasions, makes clear to the people of Israel that God is unapproachable; he is too holy for human beings to survive in his presence. Just as we cannot look directly into the sun without damaging our eyes, so God's holiness is too great for anyone to look at. I have picked out three examples of this.

In the book of Exodus, when God descends on Mount Sinai to consecrate the Israelites as his treasured possession out of all the nations,[1] Moses is warned not to let anyone set foot on the mountain.[2] God's descent is accompanied by thunder, lightning, a thick cloud and a loud trumpet blast, causing everyone in the Israelite camp to tremble.[3]

In the book of Leviticus, when Aaron and his sons are ordained as priests, the Israelites are told to prepare for the appearance of God's glory. They are instructed to offer several different elaborate animal offerings,[4] and then fire appears from nowhere and consumes the offerings on the altar.[5]

In the book of Numbers, a branch of the Levites called the Kohathites are given responsibility for the care of 'the most holy things' in the tent of meeting whenever the Israelites move camp.[6] But only after Aaron and his sons have packed up everything in the tent of meeting[7] should the Kohathites carry them to the next place. The Kohathites are warned that they must not touch the holy things, even for a moment, or they will die.[8]

The approachability of Jesus

Jesus' birth is in complete contrast to this. Prior to it, we are not told of any elaborate offerings to purify Mary. When Jesus enters the world at the end of Mary's labour, there is no thunder, lightning, cloud or trumpet blast. Mary, Joseph and the shepherds are not at risk of dying just by glancing at Jesus. Jesus humbles himself completely to be born of a woman, and is willing to be approached. He is literally Immanuel, God with us. The One who *'wraps himself in light as with a garment'* and *'stretches out the heavens like a tent'*[9] is wrapped in swaddling cloths at his birth and laid in an animal trough, where he allows himself to be looked at, touched, picked up.

Paul Brand, a pioneering hand surgeon, worked for years among people affected by the skin disease leprosy. Characteristically, sufferers lose sensation in their extremities and are often badly disfigured. But, as Paul writes, those afflicted are often viewed wrongly as being highly infectious and are therefore frequently excluded from their communities; the gift of being touched is cruelly absent in their lives. The crucial importance of touch in expressing closeness was also highlighted during the Covid restrictions, when close contact was forbidden outside of family bubbles. This absence of contact has had lasting consequences, especially for those who lost loved ones. In contrast, there was an outcry when Michelle Obama famously contravened protocol by touching Queen Elizabeth gently on her back.

God, however, knows the importance of touch, having created human beings with our five senses. In the Bible we see Jesus often touch with compassion those around him, and allow them to touch him. Many of these are considered 'unclean' by everyone else in the community[10] but Jesus wants to express his healing, love and compassion to them.

In becoming flesh, Jesus makes himself accessible, but

that also makes him vulnerable. No wonder the apostle John marvels at the fact that he and many others have seen with their own eyes the Word made flesh as he dwells among them. It is utterly astonishing!

John writes today's reading after having been an eyewitness to Jesus' death, resurrection and ascension. These three events demonstrate spectacularly that Jesus has made it possible for human beings to approach a God who up until then has been unapproachable. The temple curtain is torn in two at Jesus' death and a way into God's presence is offered. It is through the approachability of Jesus in his incarnation, and later his death, resurrection and ascension, that God the Father becomes approachable to humanity.

And that same incarnate Jesus, fully God and fully man, will one day return in glory to judge the world. How we all long to be home for Christmas! When Christ returns, we shall be, for those who have put their trust in him will be taken to be with him for ever.

1   Exodus 19:5
2   Exodus 19:12
3   Exodus 19:16
4   Leviticus 9:2–4
5   Leviticus 9:24
6   Numbers 4:4
7   Numbers 4:5–15
8   Numbers 4:20
9   Psalm 104:2
10   See, for example, Luke 8:41–56

Song: 'Christ triumphant' by Michael Saward

Name to ponder: **'Immanuel, God with us'** (Matthew 1:23)

27 DECEMBER

'Time to make your mark'

Circumcision and naming

On the eighth day, when it was time to
circumcise the child, he was named Jesus, the
name the angel had given him before he was
conceived.

LUKE 2:21

In Poland, in March 2014, metal stamps were discovered
that the SS had used to brand numbers onto prisoners in
Auschwitz concentration camp. Initially, in 1941, the left
side of the chest was used, but later the branding was
commonly moved to the left forearm. Thousands of
prisoners were given this ineradicable physical sign, a
permanent reminder to them, and to those around them,
that they had been forced to renounce ownership of their
lives. It was an utterly negative and awful sign.

In complete contrast, in the book of Genesis, God enters
into a covenant (a lasting agreement) with Abraham, the
'father' of the Jewish nation, which is to be kept for all time.
As a wholly positive sign of this covenant, Abraham's male
descendants are to carry an outward and visible mark that
they belong to God and are part of a new chosen people.
God promises to make these descendants into a nation and
to provide them with a land in which to live. The sign is that
every boy's foreskin shall be circumcised at eight days old.[1]

This procedure was of such great importance that even if the eighth day fell on the Sabbath, it should be performed. Laws prohibited work of any description on the Sabbath – even gathering wood, for example – but obedience to this covenant sign was paramount.

In our reading today, Joseph and Mary follow their people's now long-established custom. We don't know very much about the early childhood of Jesus but, following his birth in Bethlehem, the next significant events take place after only eight days when he is circumcised and officially named. There is an extraordinary point here for us to consider as the baby boy undergoes this procedure. Jesus is God's Son, so the Jews all become members of *his* family by the covenant grace of God, *his* father. However, in Jesus' extraordinary humility in becoming human, he also submits to receiving this sign, as his parents obey their covenant duty. We should pause to try to get our minds around what is happening here. Jesus is the one person who has no need to be brought into God's family and receive the blessings that come through the covenant with Abraham; he has just come down to earth from the throne of heaven. Nevertheless, he undergoes what every Jewish baby boy undergoes and so identifies himself completely and utterly with our humanity.

Circumcision as an adult is a painful procedure, by all accounts. I have been struck, though, by Sim McMillen's assertion that the most humane time to circumcise a baby is in his first month of life. Sim is a medical missionary in Africa, and a graduate of the University of Pennsylvania Medical School and the London School of Tropical Medicine. As he asserts, there needs to be sufficient time for the low levels of Vitamin K in the liver at birth to increase, thus helping the liver create the protein prothrombin which is a clotting agent of the blood. Since prothrombin levels jump to 110% of the adult level on day eight, that is the safest of all days to undergo circumcision – as our Creator God knew! Once again, the timing is important.

In the early church, when Christianity spread quickly into parts of Asia and Europe, the ritual of circumcision became a hotly debated topic. Should non-Jews be circumcised to be brought fully into the people of God, since it was an essential ritual under the covenant God made with Abraham? It fell to the apostle Paul, who spearheaded the mission to take the Christian faith to non-Jews, to argue that baptism replaced circumcision as the sign of becoming part of God's family – being another outward sign to show an inward reality of conversion and faith. Circumcision became instead a metaphor used of the heart to show commitment and obedience to God.[2] By our willing daily obedience to God, turning away from all that is not worthy of him, we signify that our hearts have been circumcised. As today we approach the new year and look back on the past year, is there anything that needs to be cut out of our lives, or anyway that we could serve God better?

Alongside the physical Jewish ritual of circumcision is the official naming of a child. Choosing a baby's name today is often thought about carefully, even agonised over, but the decision is not so commonly based on the original meaning. In fact, many people may well not know what their chosen name literally means. However, names in the Bible are hugely important because of their meaning and how they signify what the person will grow up to be. Luke has already informed us that Gabriel told Mary what name her son is to be given.[3] This detail is also in Matthew's gospel, where an angel tells Joseph that Mary's son is to be named Jesus. That angel then explains to Joseph the reason for this name: *'because he will save his people from their sins'.*[4]

We thought quite a lot during Advent itself that there is a

twin focus on Jesus' first and second comings leading up to Christmas. Perhaps today is an opportunity to reflect on what God's Son, born as a baby at Bethlehem, will grow up to be and do later in his life. I wonder whether, for many people, Jesus remains perpetually stuck in the manger, to be brought out again every year at Christmas like a Christmas decoration? If we leave him there, we miss out on the true joy and meaning of Christmas – it is full of festive celebration, yes, but more importantly it is full of joyful hope for the future because Jesus is our Saviour. He cannot save us by being born but he will save us by dying on a cross for our sins. What a precious name God gives his own Son – Jesus, God Saves, Saviour.

Here is a final thought. It is God's prerogative as Jesus' Father to give him a name, but Joseph is specifically told by the angel that he must name him Jesus. This is exactly what he does. But we might miss that by doing so, Joseph formally adopts Mary's son as his own, becoming the guardian father of Jesus. Adoption was commonplace at that time, especially in Roman society. Indeed, the emperor of the day, Caesar Augustus (of census fame), had not only been adopted – by none other than the great Julius Caesar – but also therefore had a name change. Gaius Octavius Thurinus (his birth name) became Gaius Julius Caesar Octavianus. (The senate late conferred on him the name Augustus, as we know him, meaning 'the Magnificent' or 'Venerable One', which reinforces the importance of names!)

In a similar way, the angels had announced to the shepherds that Jesus is 'the Messiah, the Lord'.[5] While 'Jesus' is the name he will be known as, his title is 'the Messiah, the Lord' because he is God's Son. There are many other magnificent names by which Jesus is called, but for now let's worship him for truly being Jesus our Saviour.

1   Genesis 17:4–12
2   Colossians 2:11–12
3   Luke 1:31
4   Matthew 1:21
5   Luke 2:11

Song: 'How sweet the name of Jesus sounds' by John Newton

Name to ponder: **'Jesus – God saves'** (Matthew 1:21)

'Bath time'

Purification

> When the time came for the purification rites
> required by the Law of Moses, Joseph and Mary
> took him to Jerusalem to present him to the
> Lord (as it is written in the Law of the Lord,
> 'Every firstborn male is to be consecrated to the
> Lord'), and to offer a sacrifice in keeping with
> what is said in the Law of the Lord: 'a pair of
> doves or two young pigeons'.
>
> LUKE 2:22–24

Exactly forty days after Mary gave birth, Luke tells us that
Mary and Joseph, in obedience to the law, travel the five
miles to Jerusalem. This is for Mary to present herself at the
vast temple (later referred to by Jesus as his Father's house[1])
for her purification. Due to the unchanging geography of the
area, we can trace Mary and Joseph's journey through the
valley from Bethlehem up the hill to Jerusalem.

We know from Matthew's gospel narrative that sometime
after Jesus' birth eminent astrologers also arrive in Jerusalem
and head straight for the palace of King Herod to enquire
about the recent birth of a king of the Jews.[2] We don't know
when the Magi arrive, later incurring the wrath of King
Herod,[3] but what is clear is God's timing and protective
provision for his Son. Meanwhile, Mary and Joseph are

oblivious to the potential danger to Jesus' life. King Herod's palace on one side backs onto the city wall, overlooking the route down the valley to the road from Bethlehem. On another side, it looks over the direct walkway from the entrance through the city wall to the temple. This area is presumably crawling with Roman soldiers. From the tower of Antonia on the corner of the temple, it is possible for soldiers to scan a full view of the temple area, with steps granting quick access. However, Joseph and Mary's journey is at this point of no apparent interest to the authorities.

This unsuspecting passing by of something of immeasurable value reminds me of another journey I read about. Weighing a breathtaking 3106 carats, a colossal diamond discovered in 1905 was initially dismissed as a shard of glass by Pretoria's premier mine inspector Frederick Wells. When its true identity was revealed, the diamond was purchased as a gift for King Edward VII. Elaborate plans were made to have the precious stone shipped to England, protected at all times by top security. However, this was later revealed to be an elaborate ruse created to fool any prospective thieves, and the stone was in fact sent to England in the post, in brown packaging with no security whatsoever!

However, there are two important reasons why their journey is necessary for the young family of Joseph, Mary and Jesus. Yesterday we thought about how Joseph and Mary followed their nation's custom of circumcision, bringing Jesus within the covenant promises made to Abraham. Today's reading tells us how the new parents fulfil some other traditional religious rites, this time according to the covenant law of Moses.

Redeeming a firstborn son is commanded in the Law as a reminder of the Israelites being spared in Egypt during the tenth and final plague when the Lord passes over the land in judgement at midnight, as we read in Exodus. The Hebrews daub blood from a sacrificed lamb on the entrance posts of their houses, denoting that they belong to God. This protects the lives of their firstborn from God's wrath, while all the Egyptian firstborn die.[4] Immediately afterwards, Moses gives this command from God to the Israelites: *'you are to give over to the LORD the first offspring of every womb … Redeem every firstborn among your sons.'*[5] The Israelites are never to forget that God has 'redeemed' them from slavery in Egypt.

Some important reflections occur to me from this. First, the blood of the lamb daubed on the doorposts points forward to Jesus' death on the cross as the 'Lamb of God' protecting us from God's wrath. Secondly, symbolically giving back a child to the Lord in gratitude is an acknowledgement that children are a precious gift from him. It reminds me of how Hannah literally does this with her son, Samuel, the great Old Testament priest and prophet, as she entrusts him as a boy to Eli in the house of the Lord in Shiloh.[6] Thirdly, the humility of Jesus also leads to complete association with his Jewish ancestry. Finally, Joseph and Mary can have only a faint glimpse of what it means for Jesus to be the One promised to redeem Israel.[7] Yet, the only perfect and sinless human being is redeemed as a baby – how extraordinary that Jesus should undergo the very rite, when he alone in the history of the human race does not need to do so!

The second part of that day's activity, Mary's purification, is part of a ritual cleansing, explained in a detailed passage in Leviticus:

> **The Lord said to Moses, 'Say to the Israelites: "A woman who becomes pregnant and gives birth to a son will be ceremonially unclean for seven days, just as she is unclean during her monthly period. On the eighth day the boy is to be circumcised.**

Then the woman must wait thirty-three days to be purified from her bleeding. She must not touch anything sacred or go to the sanctuary until the days of her purification are over ...

"When the days of her purification for a son or daughter are over, she is to bring to the priest at the entrance to the tent of meeting a year-old lamb for a burnt offering and a young pigeon or a dove for a sin offering. He shall offer them before the Lord to make atonement for her, and then she will be ceremonially clean from her flow of blood.

"These are the regulations for the woman who gives birth to a boy or a girl. But if she cannot afford a lamb, she is to bring two doves or two young pigeons, one for a burnt offering and the other for a sin offering. In this way the priest will make atonement for her, and she will be clean."[8]

Mary needs purifying from all the body fluids associated with giving birth. The verses above say that, under Jewish Law, a person in a state of uncleanliness is not permitted to touch anything sacred. Yet Jesus is sacred, so how extraordinarily gracious is God in allowing Mary, in her motherly care, to touch his Son Jesus at all, let alone when she is ritually unclean!

For those who can afford it, the Law states that a perfect lamb must be obtained and slaughtered as an offering, but different provision is made for those who cannot afford this. Mary and Joseph give two pigeons instead, confirming their poor status and the lowly family into which Jesus is born. Of course, Mary and Joseph are holding Jesus, the ultimate 'lamb' in their arms, who will later sacrifice himself for his parents and for us, just a stone's throw away from the temple.

This may seem a very ancient rite, so what relevance has it for us today? Well, we too need redeeming and purifying. Paul writes in Galatians, as we thought about at the beginning of Advent: *'But when the set time had fully come, God sent his Son, born of a woman, born under the law to redeem those under the law, that we might receive adoption to sonship.'*[9] We need purifying from our sin, and it's Jesus' blood later shed on the cross that makes us clean.[10] We can then be adopted into God's family, as his precious sons and daughters.[11]

Perhaps we can pause and consider Jesus, the great Redeemer, who gave his life as a ransom for us.[12] Do we wonder at our Lord's humility? Are we in awe that he allows us to approach him? Do we take time to thank him for redeeming us by his blood on the cross? Do we long to live today and always in a way that expresses our thanks and gratitude?

[1]   Luke 2:49
[2]   Matthew 2:1–2
[3]   Matthew 2:7–8, 12, 16
[4]   Exodus 12:21–32
[5]   Exodus 13:12–13
[6]   1 Samuel 1:27–28
[7]   Luke 1:68; 24:21
[8]   Leviticus 12:1–4, 6–8
[9]   Galatians 4:4–5
[10]   1 John 1:7–9
[11]   Ephesians 1:5
[12]   Mark 10:45

Song: 'There is a Redeemer' by Melody Green

Name to ponder: **'Redeemer'** (Psalm 78:35)

'Living on borrowed time'

Simeon

Now there was a man in Jerusalem called
Simeon, who was righteous and devout. He was
waiting for the consolation of Israel, and the
Holy Spirit was on him. It had been revealed to
him by the Holy Spirit that he would not die
before he had seen the Lord's Messiah. Moved
by the Spirit, he went into the temple courts.
When the parents brought in the child Jesus to
do for him what the custom of the Law
required, Simeon took him in his arms and
praised God, saying:

Sovereign Lord, as you have promised,
    you may now dismiss your servant in peace.
For my eyes have seen your salvation,
    which you have prepared in the sight of all
    nations:
a light for revelation to the Gentiles,
    and the glory of your people Israel.'

The child's father and mother marvelled at what
was said about him. Then Simeon blessed them
and said to Mary, his mother: 'This child is
destined to cause the falling and rising of many in
Israel, and to be a sign that will be spoken against,

so that the thoughts of many hearts will be revealed. And a sword will pierce your own soul too.'

Two American tourists once came upon Queen Elizabeth II, accompanied solely by a bodyguard, walking on her private estate in Balmoral. Engaging her in conversation, they asked if she lived nearby, little realising that she was the Queen and owned the estate. Apparently, it amused the Queen not to enlighten them and she revelled in being anonymous!

I wonder what reception Mary and Joseph imagine, if any, that they will receive bringing the Messiah to the temple in Jerusalem. Do they perhaps wonder whether there will be any recognition of Jesus from any of the temple hierarchy? How extraordinary and ironic that Jesus passes unnoticed by all but a few. Isn't it remarkable but typical how under the radar this visit is? We are only told of two significant conversations.

Today we are considering the first of these conversations, with Simeon. Probably an elderly man, he is definitely righteous and devout. The Holy Spirit has revealed to him that he will not die until he has seen the Messiah. Perhaps he was in the congregation months earlier when Zechariah reappeared dumbstruck from the Holy Place. Perhaps he recognised Zechariah when he and Elizabeth visited the temple a few months earlier with John for her purification and knows therefore that the Messiah's arrival is imminent. But we do know that Simeon is waiting for the fulfilment of a specific promise made to him by the Holy Spirit. What a feeling of wonder and celebration there will be when this long-awaited event comes to pass!

In today's reading from Luke's gospel, the Holy Spirit prompts Simeon to go into the temple courts at the very time

Mary and Joseph bring Jesus to be presented according to the Law. Perhaps Simeon's opening gambit is enquiring where the couple have travelled from today, knowing that if they answer that they have come from Bethlehem, that will indeed be a clue – for he will surely know that the city of David is where the Messiah is to be born. Perhaps he doesn't need an opening gambit because the Holy Spirit confirms to him without a shadow of a doubt whom to approach.

What a moment when, filled with emotion at the graciousness of the Lord in allowing him to receive this wonderful privilege, Simeon takes the baby Jesus into his arms! Words of praise bubble up from the Spirit and pour from Simeon's mouth in worship and gratitude to his Lord and Master – notice the title 'Sovereign' that he uses to address God. This baby, this little person hardly weighing anything in his arms, is the One – God's Messiah. Simeon takes the Son of God in his arms. What a staggering statement!

As Simeon watches this family walk away and leave the temple, he knows in his heart that God has allowed him, ordinary Simeon, the privilege and honour of seeing the Messiah. And now the Sovereign Lord can take him to rest in peace.

There are many things we could take from this reading to apply to our lives, but here are a few that have particularly struck me.

First, Simeon has been waiting to see the Lord's Messiah; he wasn't sure of the details – exactly when or where – but he has waited day after day after day. We reflected earlier in December on the Advent message of waiting patiently and obediently for Jesus' second coming. Simeon was waiting for the consolation of Israel. Are we waiting for the consolation of the world when Jesus comes again? Just because Advent is over, let's not stop remembering this!

Secondly, Simeon is obedient to the Lord's prompting, and his devotion to God enables him to listen and respond to the Holy Spirit. Do we recognise the voice of the Lord? Are we listening to him during the day, expecting his guidance and direction, and allowing the Spirit to lead us? Before we enter a room of people, or enter church, do we take a moment to ask God who he might want us to sit with to encourage, welcome or simply be a Christian presence? My parents have been a great example to me in this. They start the day by committing to God who they might meet in the supermarket aisles, in a gathering, or walking out and about. They pray that the Lord will open their eyes to see the opportunities he is giving them and the boldness to seize them.

Thirdly, Simeon's message must be completely unexpected to Mary and Joseph: their child will cause some in Israel to rise but some also to fall, and pain will come to Mary in the future. Only years later will Mary be able to look back and understand what these words mean, as she witnesses the opposition to Jesus' ministry and his eventual denouncement by the religious authorities, leading to his death. We too are graciously warned about the pain and suffering of Christian discipleship.[1] In some parts of the world this is a daily reality, even if it is not our own experience. But even for those of us not facing hostility and direct persecution, we are not promised a carefree life and need to be prepared for the challenges that will come our way.

But lastly, what a privilege it is for Simeon to see the Lord's Messiah face to face. He does not have long to live and maybe has some understanding that rather than a fleeting moment of seeing the Lord Jesus' face, it will be an everlasting one in his presence. What a privilege lies in store for all Christian believers. We won't just glimpse the face of the Saviour when we die, but are granted the honour to live with him in his house, to serve him, to worship him and to be in his presence for all eternity.[2]

1   See, for example, Acts 20:23, 29, 31; John 16:33
2   Psalm 17:15; 1 Corinthians 13:12; 2 Corinthians 3:18

Song: 'Simeon's song' by Tommy Walker

Name to ponder: **'Light of the world'** (John 8:12)

30 DECEMBER

'In the right place at the right time'

Anna

> There was also a prophet, Anna, the daughter of Penuel, of the tribe of Asher. She was very old; she had lived with her husband seven years after her marriage, and then was a widow until she was eighty-four. She never left the temple but worshipped night and day, fasting and praying. Coming up to them at that very moment, she gave thanks to God and spoke about the child to all who were looking forward to the redemption of Jerusalem.
>
> LUKE 2:36–38

As a family, we have occasionally asked God to graciously surprise one of us, if we are in particular need of encouragement due to our situation. It is thrilling how the Lord has sometimes kindly responded by an unexpected meeting with someone who was just in the right place at the right time to lift our heads and cheer us.

Our reading today follows on from yesterday's account in Luke's gospel of Jesus' presentation in the temple by Joseph and Mary. Immediately after their encounter with Simeon, they have a surprising meeting with Anna.

Anna is mentioned as a prophet, someone speaking on behalf of God, at a time when there are no known male prophets around. She is the daughter of Penuel, and I feel sure that it's not an accident that her father's name is specifically mentioned. It means 'the face of God' and is linked to the place name where Jacob wrestled with God in the book of Genesis: *'So Jacob called the place Peniel, saying, "It is because I saw God face to face, and yet my life was spared."'*[1] And, of course, Anna sees the face of God here, as she gazes upon the baby Jesus.

Although we only meet Anna in these few verses, Luke gives us a few details of her life and character. She is elderly and has been a widow for an extremely long time. Her age of eighty-four is a remarkably specific detail. I wonder whether this is because seven is a significant number in the Bible, denoting completion or perfection, as is twelve for the tribes of Israel and Jesus' selected disciples/apostles, and 84 is 7 x 12? She may well have had years of poverty, being reliant on handouts, but we don't know that for certain either. She is presumably free from ties and able to trust in the Lord to provide for her needs. She spends her life in the temple in worship and prayerful dependency on God, drawing strength and joy from being in his presence.[2] God has seen this, of course, and chooses to endow her with a special honour. Widows also have a special place in God's heart.[3] What a saint Anna must have been, exemplifying the psalmist's prayer: *'One thing I ask from the LORD, this only do I seek: that I may dwell in the house of the LORD all the days of my life, to gaze on the beauty of the LORD and to seek him in his temple.'*[4]

We also see a wonderful example of God's timing in this meeting: 'Coming up to them at that very moment', just after Simeon had given Mary a painful warning that a sword would pierce her own soul in the future. As we thought about yesterday, hearing of such a future for her son must have troubled Mary. Yet, the godly Anna is placed alongside Mary at just the right moment, to point her upwards to God and his purposes. The saving of Israel will come through her son, Jesus (even though it will at times be an extremely painful path). Anna also shares this good news with the faithful people around her. What an encouragement for them to hear this!

We might also reflect on the power of Anna's prayers in the light of John's vision in the book of Revelation: *'And when he had taken it, the four living creatures and the twenty-four elders fell down before the Lamb. Each one had a harp and they were holding golden bowls full of incense, which are the prayers of God's people.'*[5] We are told that faithful people's prayers reach right to the throne of God in heaven. I am so encouraged by people I know who are great prayer warriors like Anna.

Perhaps Anna can be an encouragement and example to us of a life lived in prayerful dependency on God. Perhaps we too could sometimes pray to be in exactly the right place at the right time to be an encouragement to others, as Anna was to Mary. And perhaps this reading reminds us to value even more the elderly in our church family, who can so often be the great prayer warriors in our midst.[6]

And lastly, consider God's thoughtfulness in the little detail of Simeon being able to share this moment with Anna. I have no doubt he would have told her of the Holy Spirit's words to him, and Anna would have kept Simeon within her view to see who he approached! How wonderful that Anna too could share in this extraordinary privilege of seeing the Messiah! Now Simeon has seen the Lord, and though he may not have many more days of his life to live, he can share them in the temple with Anna. What a typically gracious provision from the Lord. Revelation tells us that in heaven we will worship and serve God night and day.[7] Anna is completely ready to do that. I hope that we are too.

1   Genesis 32:30
2   1 Chronicles 16:27
3   Psalm 68:5
4   Psalm 27:4
5   Revelation 5:8
6   1 Thessalonians 5:17
7   Revelation 7:15

Song: 'There is a hope' by Stuart Townend

Name to ponder: **'El Channun – The gracious God'** (Jonah 4:2)

31 DECEMBER

'Time's up!'

King of the Jews ... and of the New Year

After Jesus was born in Bethlehem in Judea, during the time of King Herod, Magi from the east came to Jerusalem and asked, 'Where is the one who has been born king of the Jews?'

MATTHEW 2:1–2

Generations before the invention of mobile phones with a digital clock timer, sandglasses were commonly used to calculate the passing of time. A few centuries ago, they were used on sailing ships to measure the passing hours between crew changes. In the era of our grandparents (or even parents), they were used to time a perfectly boiled egg. Nowadays we mostly only use them in board games for timing players' turns. On this final day of the year, there is a sense of inevitability that the sands of time can't be stopped. The year will end at midnight and a new one will begin. There is nothing we can do to prevent it.

In a few hours' time there will be fireworks in the sky all over the world, with these extraordinary displays of light signalling the end of one year and the beginning of the next. So it was with the birth of the Son of God. An extremely bright light in the sky signalled the end of one era and marked the beginning of the next. Over the next few days we will be considering these events. We begin today by simply reflecting on what that great light signified to those skilled enough to read the astronomical signs.

Launched in July 2013, what3words was the brainwave of four men. Frustrated by equipment failing to turn up at the correct entrance for large-scale events, they were inspired to create a system of dividing the earth into grids of three-metre square blocks. Each block was assigned three seemingly random words as a unique address. This system provided a simple way to find and share precise locations, and has become invaluable to emergency personnel trying to locate walkers requiring assistance in remote areas.

The Magi were absolutely convinced the light in the sky indicated three words. There was nothing random about these words; they were specific. What's more, the movement of the bright light seemed to confirm them. The three words were: birth, king, Jews. From their study and knowledge of the celestial phenomena they deduced the strength, timings and position of the light denoted nothing less than the birth of a king of the Jews.

Let's briefly examine this phrase. 'King of the Jews' will recur several times later in Matthew's gospel, and he continually challenges his readers to see the truth of this claim for themselves. Although Jesus, in his adult ministry, speaks much more of the kingdom of God,[1] he demonstrates that he is the king by performing mighty deeds.[2] After three years he rides into Jerusalem to be acclaimed as the long-expected king in the line of David.[3]

Later, at his trial following his arrest, Pilate asks Jesus directly: 'Are you the king of the Jews?'[4] Where non-Jewish, highly educated Magi were in no doubt that a king had just been born, years later a non-Jewish Roman governor was perhaps curious but probably rather sceptical.

When Jesus is handed over to the Roman soldiers to be crucified, they dress him in a scarlet robe, ram a twisted crown of thorns on his head and mock him with these words: 'Hail, king of the Jews!'[5] These non-Jewish toughies could not be more cynical and sarcastic in using the phrase – although some of them, including the commanding centurion, appear to change their minds having witnessed some miraculous phenomena when Jesus dies.[6]

Finally, when Jesus is nailed naked to the cross, Pilate has an inscription placed over his head: 'THIS IS JESUS THE KING OF THE JEWS'.[7] Whether this continues the mockery heaped on Jesus or is a deliberate insult to the Jewish nation, or both, is not entirely clear, but there is no doubt that the inscription is ironic.

The beginning and end of Matthew's account of Jesus' life therefore challenges his readers to ask themselves the same question as Pilate: 'Are you the king of the Jews?' Indeed, in the light of Jesus' resurrection and the great commission to take the good news of Jesus to the ends of the earth,[8] the question for us today becomes even broader: 'Is Jesus the King of all the world?'

What will your response be? Will you put him to one side with the busyness of your New Year celebrations this evening? Or will you take time to kneel in adoration, thanking him for his awesome power and authority, for working his purposes out over the last year in your life and in the lives of those around you? Will you also trust in his plan for your life as you go into the new year, giving your allegiance again solely to him as his servant?

Today, as we sit on the cusp of the New Year, let's ponder again the significance of the night when BC turned into AD, when Jesus entered our world as a baby, when light came into the darkness. We know that the King has come and that the King will come again. Are we fully taking on board the kingship of Jesus in our lives? Are we allowing him sovereignty in every area?

As we face inevitable challenges ahead, perhaps even some uncertainty, let's remind ourselves that we don't face them alone; we go into the year with Jesus as our Lord and Saviour, putting our hand is his, the one who knows the future. Let's bow our knee to our Lord and King, the King of Kings high over all, offering to him all our obedience and worship. Let's approach the throne of grace, humbly but confidently; we are his servants, but he is our King; we are unworthy, but he is gloriously worthy.

'Yours, LORD, is the greatness and the power and the glory and the majesty and the splendour, for everything in heaven and earth is yours. Yours, LORD, is the kingdom; you are exalted as head over all.'[9]

[1]   See, for example, Matthew 6:10; 13:11, 24, 31, 33
[2]   See, for example, Matthew 4:23; 8:27; 9:8;
[3]   Matthew 21:5, 9
[4]   Matthew 27:11
[5]   Matthew 27:29
[6]   Matthew 27:54
[7]   Matthew 27:37
[8]   Matthew 28:18–20
[9]   1 Chronicles 29:11

Song: 'King of kings, Majesty' by Jarrod Cooper

Name to ponder: **'King of kings'** (Revelation 17:14)

1 JANUARY

'My times are in his hands'

Messiah

When King Herod heard this he was disturbed, and all Jerusalem with him. When he had called together all the people's chief priests and teachers of the law, he asked them where the Messiah was to be born. 'In Bethlehem in Judea,' they replied, 'for this is what the prophet has written:

"But you, Bethlehem, in the land of Judah, are by no means least among the rulers of Judah; for out of you will come a ruler who will shepherd my people Israel."'

MATTHEW 2:3–6

In September 2024, the Princess of Wales released footage of her family life. Prince George, aged eleven, was shown having fun interacting with his siblings, like any normal family. Yet when born, he became the heir's heir. Though only a baby then, too young to be capable of ruling, one day, in all probability, he will be king. The family video was all the more poignant because of the ongoing treatment the Princess of Wales is having for cancer, but how much more emotive it would be if it was also George's destiny to choose to sacrifice himself when older in order to allow his mother to go on living.

133

Yesterday we thought of Jesus, our great King; today we consider Jesus as the Messiah. Herod links the Magi's search for the king of the Jews with the Old Testament prophecies of a Messiah, which is why he calls the chief priests and teachers of the law. They immediately quote Micah's prophecy that Bethlehem will be his birthplace.[1] The Greek word translated 'Messiah' is 'Christos' (often translated 'Christ') meaning 'Anointed One'. But what was their understanding of this term, and what did Jesus himself go on to explain and then demonstrate that it really meant?

Last month we examined a handful of prophecies concerning the Messiah. These signs would help the people recognise him when he came. Jesus ticked the boxes of being born to a virgin, of the right heritage and with the time and place of his birth aligned. But the Jewish nation assumed that the coming Messiah, being God's king, would save them from Roman rule. Rather than looking at the full picture of all the prophecies, they were looking for how the Messiah would resolve their present predicament by freeing them from the Romans' hold on them, in a blaze of power, honour and glory.

But as Jesus' ministry progressed, and the disciples came to believe that he really was the Messiah, Jesus indicated very clearly that this meant that he had to suffer. Later in Matthew's gospel, when Peter boldly affirms that Jesus is the Christ, the disciples are then taught that he must go to Jerusalem to die.[2]

His earthly father, Joseph, had been told that Jesus would save God's people from their sins[3] and Jesus confirms at the start of his adult ministry that he has come to save sinners.[4] Jesus later explains that he will do this by giving up his life as a ransom for many.[5]

The disciples are so surprised, and indeed upset, when Jesus explains that he *must* die. Yet those who knew the

Scriptures well should have understood from passages such as Isaiah 53 that the Messiah had to suffer. His punishment and his wounds would be the means of healing, and he would be cut off from the land of the living.[6] This was confirmed by Daniel's prophecy that the Anointed One would be 'put to death'.[7] Other Old Testament prophecies about the Messiah used words that described anything but glory – words such as those in Psalm 22: 'forsaken', 'cries of anguish', 'scorned', 'despised', 'poured out', 'in the dust of death'.[8]

These words describe in uncanny detail the events of the last hours of Jesus' life leading up to his crucifixion. So many of them are direct prophecies, using the exact words and circumstances that occurred.

Jesus was despised and mocked by the Roman soldiers,[9] as well as by people who revelled in the opportunity to get back at him for what they saw as him letting them down. He was scorned for stating that he was the Son of God, as they considered this the height of blasphemy.[10] They ridiculed Jesus, telling him to come down from the cross and save himself.[11] His garments, such as they were, were divided among the soldiers casting lots.[12]

Psalm 22 finishes with the words 'He has done it!'[13] These correspond amazingly with Jesus' cry as he took his last breath on the cross: 'It is finished.'[14] The same Greek word was stamped on documents of that time when a debt had been paid, signifying the repayment was completed.

Many young people of this generation are carrying a financial debt for years, maybe because they are paying off a student loan or having to live beyond their means for a period of time. Others have a lifetime mortgage which is always there, though being paid off bit by bit. What joy there is when these debts are paid, finished, dealt with, no more. There's a freedom and something refreshing about the new start paying off a debt brings.

At the start of this new year, let's remind ourselves that if we have claimed Jesus' death for ourselves, this is what Jesus our Saviour offers us once more. Let this fact lead us to gratitude, praise and a motivation to serve him and others as an expression of that thankfulness. We have a gospel of good news to share, so let's head into this New Year keeping the cross central to our thinking.

1   Micah 5:2
2   Matthew 16:21
3   Matthew 1:21
4   Mark 2:7
5   Mark 10:45
6   Isaiah 53:5, 8
7   Daniel 9:26
8   Psalm 22:1, 6, 14–15
9   Matthew 27:29
10 Matthew 27:43
11 Matthew 27:40
12 John 19:23–24
13 Psalm 22:31
14 John 19:30

Song: 'Behold him' by Paul Baloche

Name to ponder: **'Messiah'** (Matthew 2:4)

2 JANUARY

'Time bomb'

Herod

After Jesus was born in Bethlehem in Judea, during the time of King Herod, Magi from the east came to Jerusalem and asked, 'Where is the one who has been born king of the Jews? We saw his star when it rose and have come to worship him.'

When King Herod heard this he was disturbed, and all Jerusalem with him. When he had called together all the people's chief priests and teachers of the law, he asked them where the Messiah was to be born. 'In Bethlehem in Judea,' they replied, 'for this is what the prophet has written:

"But you, Bethlehem, in the land of Judah,
are by no means least among the rulers of
Judah; for out of you will come a ruler
who will shepherd my people Israel."

Then Herod called the Magi secretly and found out from them the exact time the star had appeared. He sent them to Bethlehem and said, 'Go and search carefully for the child. As soon as you find him, report to me, so that I too may go and worship him.'

MATTHEW 2:1–8

In September 2024 it was reported in the press that Kim Jong Un, supreme leader of North Korea, ordered the executions of up to thirty officials, apparently because they failed to prevent flooding that had led to widespread death. Since taking power in 2011 he is reported to have executed his uncle and ordered his brother-in-law to be killed for an attempted coup. North Korea isn't just a very dangerous place for officials, but for believers too: for twenty years it has been at or near the top of the Open Doors world watch list for persecuted Christians. To be discovered as a believer can lead to either on-the-spot execution or exportation to labour camp. Kim Jong Un is just one example out of many modern-day dictators, all of whom hold great power and often record great achievements but act with utter ruthlessness to retain their position.

King Herod of Judea could rightly be called 'great' in terms of his political governance, war record and building achievements. Some remains of the buildings he commissioned still exist today: the port at Caesarea, built in honour of the Roman emperor at the time, Caesar Augustus; his palace on the mountain of Masada, which is still a popular tourist attraction; and the retaining walls (including the western wall) of the rebuilt temple in Jerusalem. Judea can certainly be said to have prospered in worldly terms during Herod's reign.

In our passage today, the Magi arrive in Jerusalem with their entourage of accompanying attendants. They ask around, initially at the palace (the obvious place for a king to be born), where they should go to find the new king of the Jews.

Expecting to find Jerusalem rejoicing, the Magi instead discover that everyone is unaware of such an important birth. Herod gets to hear of their mission and is 'disturbed', presumably through fear of being overthrown by this new

Jewish king he knows nothing about. If ancient sources are to be believed, 'disturbed' might be a euphemism for 'incandescent with rage'; the historian Josephus often refers to Herod's temper and his fear of being overthrown.[1] Perhaps Herod is also caught off guard by what appears to be an embassy from outside the Roman Empire coming to pay their respects to the new baby heir.

Then Herod gathers all the chief priests, teachers and scribes, whose job is to interpret and teach the law, and asks them where the Christ is to be born. They have no hesitation in replying categorically that it is to be in Bethlehem in Judea, which is only about six miles away. Knowing the risks of giving a wrong answer, it's unlikely that they would have given this reply unless they were absolutely sure, but then Micah's prophecy years before could not have been any clearer.[2]

When Herod seeks a private audience with the Magi, he extracts from them the exact time that the light they saw in the sky first appeared. He alleges that he wishes to worship this new king himself and asks the Magi to go to Bethlehem and search for the child. This is exactly the same phrase Matthew later uses when Judas comes to betray Jesus in the garden of Gethsemane; going 'to worship' can also be translated going 'to draw near to kiss'.[3] In both instances the implied action is deceitful. Herod has no intention of worshipping Jesus, and his desire to eradicate any threat to his rule or his successors has terrible repercussions for the children known to have been born in the Bethlehem area at the same time.[4]

Matthew's presentation of Herod's behaviour as king, supported by other ancient historical sources, could not be in greater contrast to the kingship of Jesus. Jesus turned the world's idea of greatness on its head, saying *'whoever wants to become great among you must be your servant'*.[5] His reign is one of servant-heartedness, justice and compassion, of wisdom and righteousness, of healing and wholeness. He is awesome in his power but trustworthy in his exercise of it. Jesus is the same yesterday, today and for ever;[6] we need feel no unpredictability. He knows all his subjects by name and knows all about us.[7] We are his heirs,[8] freely sharing in his riches, which he delights to give us. In return, as we seek to follow his example, can we not willingly submit to him, giving up our lives for him who gave up his for us, and offer ourselves in his service all our days?

Herod tried to destroy baby Jesus, but as Jesus would go on to say in his adult life, no one can take his life; it is for him to lay down at the exact time of his choosing.[9] Nothing can thwart God's plans. I don't think it is too far-fetched to see Herod as Satan's tool to try to destroy Jesus. Likewise, throughout history, Satan has sought to destroy God's followers by various ways and means. We need to be aware of our enemy. Satan prowls around looking for someone to devour.[10] We must be on our guard against him and his ways. We must stand firm in the Lord, equipped with the armour of God.[11]

We need to pray for world leaders and their advisors, however ruthless and fearsome they may be. God can raise up believers in their inner circle just as there was a believer, Joanna, married to the household manager of Herod's son, Herod Antipas![12] Let's pray for Christians to be given strategic positions in leadership. At the same time, how much do we need to pray for our fellow believers in countries such as North Korea, where the cost of believing in Christ is so great.

Herod didn't want anyone else to wear his crown. Neither do we. We all want to keep control over our own lives rather than surrender authority to Jesus the King. That is something to ponder when we open our crackers over any late Christmas celebrations and place paper crowns on our heads!

Ignorance and pain at wounded pride can sometimes lead to irritability at least and to rage and violence at worst. Here Herod's fury was so terrible that 'all Jerusalem' knew. His temper had horrendous consequences on the lives of the families in Bethlehem. Is a temper something we struggle with? Does everyone around us know when we've been crossed? Let's not give Satan a foothold but *'take captive every thought to make it obedient to Christ.'*[13]

What a contrast there is between the earthly ruler Herod and the heavenly King we worship. How worthy of our praise God is![14]

[1]   See, for example, Josephus' *Antiquities of the Jews* 16:8.2
[2]   Micah 5:2
[3]   Matthew 26:48–50
[4]   Matthew 2:16
[5]   Matthew 20:26
[6]   Hebrews 13:8
[7]   Isaiah 43:1
[8]   Romans 8:16–17
[9]   John 10:18
[10] 1 Peter 5:8
[11] Ephesians 6:11–12
[12] Luke 8:3
[13] 2 Corinthians 10:5
[14] 1 Chronicles 16:25, 27

'The Servant King' by Graham Kendrick

Name to ponder: **'Servant King'** (*based* on Mark 10:45)

3 JANUARY

'Time to go'

The Magi

Magi from the east came to Jerusalem and
asked, 'Where is the one who has been born
king of the Jews? We saw his star when it rose
and have come to worship him.'

MATTHEW 2:1–2

People will travel considerable distances for a significant
occasion. When Queen Elizabeth II died at Balmoral on 8
September 2022, literally hundreds of thousands of people
paid homage to her leading up to her funeral at Westminster
Abbey on 19 September. People travelled from all over the
world to walk past her body lying in state, first in Edinburgh
and then in Westminster Hall, London. The vast majority of
these people had never met her, but they revered her and
wanted to honour her by paying their respects. The queue to
file past her coffin was at times said to be nearly ten miles
long, and the wait for some people more than twenty-four
hours.

Yesterday, we thought about one of the important characters in chapter 2 of Matthew's account, namely King
Herod. Today, we are considering the other main characters,
the Magi. They had travelled presumably some distance to
reach Jerusalem in order to acknowledge not the death but
the birth of a monarch.

When Matthew refers to 'Magi', what might he have wanted to convey, what might his readers have understood and what relevance could that possibly have for us today? Matthew is clearly steeped in the Old Testament – he regularly uses quotations from it as he writes his account – so let's look at a few examples to get an idea of what this term meant.

In the book of Genesis, there are advisors and 'wise men' in Pharoah's court who are unable to interpret Pharoah's dream. However, when Joseph is called up from his cell to interpret it, he is able to do so.[1] In Exodus, again in Egypt, we read of a group of magicians who are able to mimic Moses' and Aaron's initial miraculous deeds but are then unable to match their following exploits.[2] However, it is in the book of Daniel that 'magi' appear in a similar group of 'wise men', acting as advisors to the kings of Babylon. It is no coincidence that this group includes those who can interpret dreams and those who can perform magical feats because that is part of what royal advisors needed to be able to do.[3] (They also advised on points of law and custom, recalled examples from their national traditions and literature, and interpreted signs that occurred, including celestial phenomena.)

Daniel, an exile from Judah, has himself become one of these 'wise men', having far excelled his peers during his education and training in the Babylonian customs and literature.[4] This group is summoned first by Nebuchadnezzar and then by Belshazzar to interpret their respective supernatural experiences. Nebuchadnezzar has had a dream;[5] Belshazzar has seen a hand writing on the wall during a feast.[6] Both demand interpretations from their advisors, but only Daniel is able to do this for them. Nebuchadnezzar rewards Daniel by making him chief of all the 'wise men' in his kingdom;[7] Belshazzar makes him the third most powerful man in the kingdom.[8] There are striking echoes of Joseph's life in Egypt. Having correctly interpreted that Pharoah's dream was about a terrible famine to come, Joseph was elevated to the equivalent of prime minister to prepare for it.[9]

The Magi referred to in our reading today would have led Matthew's original Jewish readers to think of these Old Testament examples. They are highly educated men, whose particular expertise is in interpreting celestial phenomena. At the end of this specific account, they are given guidance in their own dream not to report back to Herod but to return home by an alternative route.[10]

It is certainly possible that these Magi might have been educated in the traditions and customs of a royal court 'in the east', including traditions about Daniel. We know that many Jews remained in the Persian Empire while some returned to Jerusalem. Might some of them also have handed down these memories or even been influential in the royal court?

This is, of course, speculation, but the book of Daniel does contain some extraordinary prophecies about the coming of a Jewish Messiah. That Nebuchadnezzar's dream mentioned this is highly significant. Daniel is able to tell the king precisely what his dream is, as well as its interpretation. One part of his interpretation is that the God of heaven will set up a kingdom that will never be destroyed; it will be a kingdom that will last for ever.[11]

Sometime later, Daniel had a vision of his own that foretold something similar but this time focused on the king who would reign:

In my vision at night I looked, and there before me was one like a son of man, coming with the clouds of heaven. He approached the Ancient of Days and was led into his presence. He was given authority, glory and sovereign power; all nations and peoples of every language worshipped him. His dominion is an everlasting dominion that will not pass away, and his kingdom is one that will never be destroyed.[12]

Was this what the Magi also had in mind when they came searching for the one born king of the Jews?

Here is another example of God's immaculate timing. God guided the Magi very clearly to where he wanted them, when he wanted. His timing was utterly perfect. He placed the star exactly where he desired in the heavens, at exactly the time he intended, causing the Magi to prepare and set off weeks, possibly months, before Jesus' birth. They had to arrive in Bethlehem after Jesus had been born but before Joseph and Mary thought of returning home to Nazareth. That was a very narrow window!

Some come to a personal encounter with Jesus through intellectual interest; others have a 'light-bulb' moment; for others it's a gradual realisation that the gospel message is true. We all have our own story. Are we prepared to share it as we head into another year, and use it to encourage others to come to know the Lord Jesus for themselves? Let's pray for an opportunity to do so!

God says through the prophet Jeremiah that we will find him if we seek him with all our hearts.[13] Wise men sought Jesus; they still do.

1   Genesis 41:14–38
2   Exodus 7:10–12, 20–22; 8:6–7, 17–18
3   Daniel 2:2
4   Daniel 1:19–20
5   Daniel 2:3
6   Daniel 5:5
7   Daniel 2:48
8   Daniel 5:29
9   Genesis 41:39–44
10 Matthew 2:12
11 Daniel 2:44
12 Daniel 7:13–14
13 Jeremiah 29:13

Song: 'Be still for the presence of the Lord' by David J. Evans

Name to ponder: **'Wonderful Counsellor'** (Isaiah 9:6)

'Potentate of time'

The star

'We saw his star when it rose and have come to worship him.'
… the star they had seen when it rose went ahead of them until it stopped over the place where the child was. When they saw the star, they were overjoyed.

MATTHEW 2:2, 9–10

Two NASA astronauts fixing a panel on an international space station accidentally dropped their toolbox. On 21 November 2023 the tabloids claimed that a bright light akin to a slow moving star would be visible through binoculars or telescopes as the toolbox flew past in the sky on its way to who knows where. Apparently the toolbox joins a spatula and a glove also inadvertently dropped and floating somewhere in the ether!

When my eldest daughter was planning how she and her husband would leave for their honeymoon, she broached the idea of guests creating an archway by holding sparklers to light up the darkness. In order to establish how dark it would be at the time they intended to leave, I was able to look up months in advance what time, to the minute, the sun would set on that particular day.

Using historical records and computer simulations from

the angle of Babylon in Iraq, it is possible to go back in time to look at various signs in the sky which the Magi might have seen if they had come from Persia. There are several fascinating scenarios dating to around the time of Herod's death. Some of them mention specific movement relating to Pisces, Jupiter and/or Saturn.

Astronomers thought movement in Pisces marked the end of one period and the beginning of the new. Jupiter was established as the brightest and 'king' of the planets. It is sometimes active in the constellation of Leo, the Lion, the animal sign for the tribe of Judah or the Jewish nation. Saturn also had strong associations with Israel because of its link with Saturday, the Jewish Sabbath.

Activity in specific areas at specific times, or combinations of movement or even a supernova convinces the Magi that the light they had seen rise told of the birth of a king to the Jewish nation. They are so elated at their findings that they feel compelled to follow the light to its destination. The phrase for their reaction in our reading today is understated in the New International Version translation; the original Greek says that when the star finally stopped over where Jesus was, they 'rejoiced exceedingly with great joy'.

Over a millennium previously, Balaam was divinely inspired to prophesy that a new star would signal the rising of a great king in Israel: *'I see him, but not now; I behold him, but not near. A star will come out of Jacob; a sceptre will rise out of Israel.'*[1] It should therefore be no great surprise that God uses a dramatic light in the sky to indicate that something very significant has happened on earth.

Going back even further, the book of Genesis, in a wonderful understatement, states that God also made the stars and that the lights in the heavens were created for signs: *'And God said, "Let there be lights in the vault of the sky to separate the day from the night, and let them serve as signs to mark sacred times, and days and years.'* [2]

Just as God used something highly appropriate, an animal food trough, as a sign to the shepherds, so he uses a sign that the Magi recognise from their area of expertise: a celestial phenomenon.

There are other examples in both the Old and New Testaments when God used unusual sightings in the heavens for significant events. We read of a pillar of fire guiding the Israelites by night through the wilderness;[3] the sun standing still in answer to Joshua's prayer;[4] and darkness over the whole land for three hours when Jesus died[5] – a fact prophesied by the prophet Amos hundreds of years before.[6] Just as a light signalled his birth, darkness accompanied his death. For these signs to occur in the heavens, yet again God's timing was exact.

Two thousand years later, we, like the Magi, desire to be guided to Jesus. We long to honour and adore him, to know his will and to seek his presence. How can we know the way to Jesus in the absence of a specific bright light in our daily lives? The psalmist says that God's word is a lamp to our feet and a light to our paths.[7] We have the privilege of access to the words that Jesus himself spoke and the accounts of what he did, enabling us to come into a deeper relationship with him for ourselves. Do we value his words as sweeter than honey[8] and as a prime source of guidance in our twenty-first-century lives? Some of our fellow Christians in other parts of the world only own parts of the Bible or have to memorise verses or passages; we must make good use of our free access to it, and treasure that freedom. We have a wonderful promise in one of the proverbs: *'in all your ways submit to him, and he will make your paths straight.'*[9]

For a God who is light[10] this isn't a surprise. His light shines in the darkness and is available to everyone.[11] Let's pray for those around us walking in darkness, and let the light of the Lord Jesus living in us shine out to others.[12]

1   Numbers 24:17
2   Genesis 1:14
3   Joshua 10:12–14
4   Exodus 13:21
5   Luke 23:44–45
6   Amos 8:9
7   Psalm 119:105
8   Psalm 119:103
9   Proverbs 3:6
10   1 John 1:5
11   John 1:9
12   Matthew 5:16

Song: 'Star Carol' by John Rutter

Name to ponder: **'The light of the world'** (John 8:12)

5 JANUARY

'No time like the present'

The Magi's gifts

**Then they opened their treasures and presented
him with gifts of gold, frankincense and myrrh.**

MATTHEW 2:11

It can sometimes be tricky to know what gift to give for an occasion or to mark a specific milestone. We want to give something that will please, but sometimes hesitate wondering whether it would give us pleasure to receive rather than being to the taste of the recipient. Years ago, for our wedding, my husband and I were given five crystal bowls. They were all very beautiful, but we only really have use for one of them and that is not very often. I imagine that's why gift lists for weddings came into vogue!

What would a suitable gift be for a king or queen? Our own royal family, apparently, often give humorous or personalised presents to each other. One of the first gifts that Catherine, Princess of Wales, gave to her then new mother-in-law was her own homemade chutney.

Our reading today continues on from yesterday's passage as the Magi finally reach Bethlehem. They have followed the star's progress in the sky until it stops over the place where Jesus is. There is no case of mistaken identity here. The Magi are totally convinced that Jesus, in his humble lodging, is the baby king they are looking for, and they are filled with exuberant gladness and delight. Their response is to fall down and worship him, and to offer the gifts that they have brought with them.

The Magi are confident that the sign they had seen in the sky signifies not just the birth of an important person but the birth of a king, specifically the king of the Jews. They therefore take gifts suitable for a king: gold, frankincense and myrrh – all costly and rare commodities. These are worthy as a royal offering, and surely never to be given to the wrong person! It is often said that these gifts represent not just kingship, but priesthood and death as well. Perhaps Matthew intends his readers to think of all these associations, but this Old Testament prophecy may well have been in the forefront of his mind too: *'Nations will come to your light, and kings to the brightness of your dawn … bearing gold and incense and proclaiming the praise of the LORD.'*[1]

It is unsurprising that gold is one of the gifts. It was a scarce and beautiful metal, often associated with royalty as well as deity. The holy of holies, the innermost and holiest place in the temple in Jerusalem where God dwelt, was adorned with lavish amounts of gold. For example, the ark of the covenant was overlaid with gold, on top of which was placed the atonement cover of solid gold.[2] King Solomon is brought gold as a gift by sailors sent by Hiram, King of Tyre,[3] and perhaps even more strikingly, also by the Queen of Sheba. We read of her *arriving at Jerusalem with a very great caravan – with camels carrying spices, large quantities of gold, and precious stones*[4]

Frankincense, being an ingredient for an aromatic incense, is associated with holiness, as when Moses meets with God in the tent of meeting.[5] King David asks the Lord that his prayer be counted as incense before him.[6] In the book of Revelation there is this beautiful symbolic picture: *'golden bowls full of incense, which are the prayers of the saints'*.[7] Yet, as with gold, frankincense is also considered an appropriate gift for kings or those of high status. When Daniel is able to interpret the king of Babylon's dream, unlike the other court advisors, Nebuchadnezzar honours him by presenting him with incense.[8]

Myrrh was used together with other ingredients as a sacred anointing oil, as God dictated its usage to Moses.[9] By repeatedly 'wounding' a branch of the shrub, which is covered in hideous thorns, tears of precious liquid resin form. It is an appropriate property of myrrh that these 'tears' can provide healing for wounds and bruises. How apt is this beautiful visual illustration of Jesus being pierced for our transgressions so that by his wounds we are healed.[10] The Jewish nation embalmed the bodies of their dead with myrrh, so we read that Jesus' dead body was lavishly embalmed with a mixture of aloes and myrrh.[11] However, as with frankincense, myrrh can also just be seen as an appropriate gift to give to a king, an expensive and extravagant ointment.

What costly gifts, worthy of a newborn king, the Magi bring to the infant Jesus, and with what great honour and worship they present them!

We have just celebrated Christmas, the season for giving gifts, and no doubt we have given and received a number ourselves. But what gifts can we bring to Jesus today?

In one sense, there is nothing we can give that is worthy of or holy enough for him. But we can give our humble worship, our time and our obedience, finding out what pleases the Lord.[12] And we can offer him our God-given talents and abilities. We may be able to offer some of our financial resources to support our local church or Christian missionary organisations. God loves a cheerful giver.[13]

If we know that we really don't have very much to offer Jesus, we can take reassurance by how just a few loaves and fish were used by him to great effect;[14] and how a widow was commended for her temple offering to God of the only small coins she owned.[15] So let us not neglect to do good and to share what we have, *'for with such sacrifices God is pleased'*.[16]

1   Isaiah 60:3, 6
2   Exodus 25:10–18
3   1 Kings 9:27–28
4   1 Kings 10:2
5   Exodus 30:34–37
6   Psalm 141:2
7   Revelation 5:8
8   Daniel 2:46
9   Exodus 30:22–25
10   Isaiah 53:5, 1 Peter 2:24
11   John 19:38–40
12   Ephesians 5:10
13   2 Corinthians 9:7
14   John 6:9–11
15   Luke 21:2
16   Hebrews 13:16

Song: 'O worship the Lord in the beauty of holiness' by J.S.B. Monsell

Name to ponder: **'His indescribable gift'** (2 Corinthians 9:15)

6 JANUARY

'Time of worship'

Now and for all eternity

On coming to the house, they saw the child with his mother Mary, and they bowed down and worshipped him.

MATTHEW 2:11

A few years ago, we set off by car on a family holiday to visit another family near to the border of the Czech Republic with Poland. We had their address and the modern aids of a road map and sat nav on our phones, but it was still going to be a long journey through England, France, Belgium and Germany. This would be the first time our daughters had seen again the woman who had looked after them for several months as a live-in au pair after our car accident. The anticipation grew on the way, since she now had a family of her own, whom we had never met. We eventually reached their home ten days later, after driving well over a thousand miles. We had a wonderful time catching up on all that had happened since the accident, and our daughters were able to convey their gratitude for all that she had done for them.

Over the last few days of our Bible reflections, we have looked at the Magi's visit to Jerusalem, their journey to Bethlehem and the royal gifts they had brought with them to give to the newborn king. Today, as we come to the end of these devotional readings from Advent to Epiphany, let's enter into the sense of awe that the Magi must have felt as they reached the goal of all their endeavours. They had told Herod that the motivation for their long journey, following a star, was to find the king of the Jews so that they could worship him. Now that moment has arrived. They have reached Bethlehem and found a mother with her infant child. So, what do they do next? *'They bowed down and worshipped him.'*

It is difficult to convey the extraordinary significance of this moment. After days of anticipation, the Magi now have their own private audience with Jesus. Consider the account of Moses coming face to face with God, which caused his face to become so radiant that it had to be veiled so as not to blind his fellow Israelites.[1] Or that of Peter, James and John witnessing the transfiguration of Jesus up a mountain.[2] But there is no blinding light mentioned here. There is just a child with his mother. Yet, it is no less an awesome moment in time. God has, for the first and only time in human history, become incarnate; God has become human. So 'they bowed down and worshipped him.'

The Magi then return home, their mission accomplished. They have no idea what will become of this baby, what he will grow up to do as an adult. They have received nothing from him, and will probably not see him again or hear anything he says or teaches. But seeing him just that once was surely enough and a moment they would never forget. These Magi teach us the importance of doing everything we can to find Jesus, to seek the pearl of great price,[3] giving everything we can to find it. They also demonstrate that having found Jesus, it is right to bow down and worship him. The following chorus line captures something of the awesomeness: 'Turn your eyes upon Jesus, look full in his wonderful face, and the things of earth will grow strangely dim, in the light of his glory and grace'.[4]

6 January is a big celebration day in many countries, when gifts are given to family and friends in honour of the Magi bringing their gifts to Jesus. It is a good day to consider whether we are filled with awe and wonder at what the Lord has done for us. It is also an opportune time to reflect back over Advent and Christmas and to remember that Jesus, who came the first time as a baby to save humanity, will return a second time to judge us and to take his people to be with him for ever.

It was promised in the Old Testament that the Messiah would come, and he did in God's perfect timing. It is promised in the New Testament that Jesus will come again in God's perfect timing, and Christians believe that he will. The Magi were the first people to worship Jesus at his first coming. On the great day at his second coming, every knee will bow and every tongue confess that Jesus Christ is Lord. What inexpressible joy we will have when Jesus returns!

Michael Fish will forever be remembered for his BBC weather forecast at 1 p.m. on 15 October 1987, when he failed to warn of severe winds arriving that night. He mentioned that the BBC had received a call from a lady who was concerned a hurricane was on the way, but urged his callers not to worry. He said the winds concerned would concentrate over Spain and France, bringing heavy rain eventually over south-east England. Although not technically classed as a hurricane, there were nevertheless winds of around 120 mph that night, causing eighteen people to be killed, fifteen million trees to be flattened and havoc around the country.

We can't say that we haven't been warned about Jesus' second coming. Met Office predictions about heavy rain can lead to precautionary action by some but a laissez-faire attitude in others. Unfortunately, the latter isn't an option with Jesus' return. When he comes, it will be too late to begin considering Jesus and his claims; the deliberation needs to be done now. With warnings about extreme weather, we even know something of the expected time when it will strike. In stark contrast, we do not know the timing of Jesus' return. Instead, we are warned not to be caught unawares like a homeowner burgled at night.[5] Will you be ready?

Let's finish with a wonderful glimpse into heaven seen by John and written in the last book of the Bible. It reveals the unending worship of Jesus by countless people, of all generations down the years and across the world, as they witness his glory for themselves face to face:

> After this I looked, and there before me was a great multitude that no one could count, from every nation, tribe, people and language, standing before the throne and before the Lamb. They were wearing white robes and were holding palm branches in their hands. And they cried out in a loud voice:
>
> 'Salvation belongs to our God,
> who sits on the throne,
> and to the Lamb.'
>
> All the angels were standing round the throne and round the elders and the four living creatures. They fell down on their faces before the throne and worshiped God, saying:
>
> 'Amen!
> Praise and glory
> and wisdom and thanks and honour
> and power and strength
> be to our God for ever and ever.
> Amen!'[6]

Maranatha, Come Lord Jesus!

1. Exodus 34:35
2. Matthew 17:1–2
3. Matthew 13:45–46
4. Taken from the hymn 'Turn your eyes upon Jesus' by Helen Howarth Lemmel
5. Matthew 24:42–44
6. Revelation 7:9–12

Song: 'Hymn of heaven' by Phil Wickham

Name to ponder: **'Alpha and Omega'** (Revelation 1:8)

APPENDIX

'Time to reflect'

When I look back at the sequence of events leading up to our accident in February 1999, I have always been totally convinced of, and overwhelmed by, the Lord's hand over that period. He seemed to have planned every intricate detail as well as the big picture. It has given me enormous comfort and reassurance to know that he was totally in control of that whole event, which was permitted yet filtered through his hands.

David was a housemaster of sixty-seven boys at one of a school's boarding houses. Located in the countryside just outside Reading, we, and the entire community of staff and pupils, lived on site. Our two children, aged four and three, were fortunately tucked up in bed fast asleep in the care of babysitters when we left the house that evening to go for a meal with some friends. We had no idea that it would be nearly two months until I could return home, although David was able to leave hospital after four weeks.

Our boarding house was beautiful and large, and had a private area with ample accommodation attached. This was to prove indispensable in the following months to accommodate the various people who came to look after us all, most notably my parents (who in the end stayed for six months!) and my mother-in-law (who gave my parents a break when she could). David and I were very restricted in managing everyday life on our return from hospital, and a live-in au pair was essential to look after our children full-time.

We also had the provision of a flat at the top of the boarding house, in which a tutor could stay to look after the overnight supervision aspect of David's job. We were part of a very supportive community, and cleaning and central catering was available, which relieved my parents of the burden of having to provide this.

We were additionally blessed with lovely wide door posts enabling easy access for a wheelchair. A long corridor upstairs enabled me to wheel along to see the children in their bedroom (although it had an adverse camber!), when I was able to do that on my own. The school provided a ramp outside the back of our house, which enabled me to use the wheelchair out on the patio and enjoy the garden – something I had missed very much when being confined (literally, attached!) to the hospital bed.

A few months before our accident, in November 1998, my father retired from his extremely busy job as a rector in a parish in Devon. The timing was another gigantic provision, as his ministry (together with my mother's) had been more than full-time for many, many years, but they were now free to move in with us. Previously, they had rarely been able to visit us. Then, just five weeks earlier, they had spent Christmas with us and therefore had seen some of our routines. Our girls had become used to being with them, which was to prove extremely important for their emotional welfare over the next few months.

Our accident happened one evening at the beginning of February when, shortly after leaving home, we were hit head on by a drunk driver driving fast towards us on our side of the road in a dark country lane. Yet God had already set in motion a whole string of circumstances which would make a great deal of difference to the weeks and months in the aftermath of the collision.

God ensured too, in his wonderful timing, who should be

in a car also travelling along that road, arriving at a similar time albeit from the opposite direction. Out of all the people it could have been, it was the head of the A&E department at a leading hospital in the area! Not only that, but he was accompanied by his son who was a pupil at our school, so knew exactly who we were – even in the dark country lane. We had the best people in place to set events in motion – what a provision! The father was able to call for the emergency services required, which in our case was several fire engines, police cars and ambulances crowding into the country lane.

Having been the first to come out of unconsciousness, I was imploring God to save David's life. I could see him slumped over the steering wheel next to me, apparently not breathing and completely unresponsive.

Meanwhile, the consultant's son contacted someone at school, who in turn contacted the senior management team, who 'happened' to choose a Christian friend of ours to tell. He dashed from his home to come to us, but first told his wife the situation. She 'happened' to belong to my local Bible study group and phoned the first person on our prayer chain, who immediately alerted the others. They were all able to pray for us while we were still trapped in the car. When I asked our friend, who was standing near the wreckage, to inform my prayer chain, he was able to tell me that they were already praying! While I was being cut out of the car, this was of immense value and relief to me. Knowing that my friends were at that moment interceding on my behalf for David enabled me to concentrate on the instructions the medics and fire service officers were giving me. What an unbelievable privilege to have that support. What a great God. What precious friends.

Our heavenly Father had also ensured that another family friend was alerted by the house tutor to stay overnight, relieving the boys who were babysitting. In addition, my brother Richard came straight from the squash courts in London, alerted by his wife Joy, who our friend had already contacted.

Unbeknown to me at the time, another of our friends was enduring her own trauma, having to undergo a stillbirth. Our vicar was already at the hospital supporting her and her husband. When yet another friend phoned the boarding house to let me know about this sad situation, she was told by the tutor on duty that we had had a car crash and were being taken to hospital. She then contacted the vicar's wife, who immediately got a message to her husband at the hospital. The vicar was able to pray with me for David, once I'd been released from the resuscitation room (after the staff had had to cut off some favourite clothes I had been wearing). This prayer time meant a great deal since I gathered that David was still unresponsive and was also undergoing a brain scan. What an extraordinary chain of events to have in motion!

I knew pretty quickly that my feet were injured, and it wasn't long before I discovered just how badly they had been damaged. A while later on the ward, I was told that it was possible that I might not even be able to walk again. Yet months later I was able to start mobilising, and years later I could walk freely in trainers. This recovery was to give even more glory to God.

The rod that was put through one of my heels in theatre to stabilise the fractures was smooth not threaded, as it should have been so as not to slip. I was completely flat on my back for a month, with no option of lying in different positions due to that leg being in traction, the other being in heavy plaster and with me also having a fractured arm. I could lift my hip slightly up to the left or right, but the rod would gradually slip out of place in my heel. In order for it to be repositioned, it would be attached to a T-bar and physically pulled through my heel every day for four weeks. This was unbelievably excruciating, and caused me enormous distress, until an anaesthetist – who 'happened' to be passing and who I 'happened' to have met once at toddler group – suggested Entonox (gas and air) should be used. That made an extraordinary difference.

The recovery in hospital was a terrible experience for me, for many different reasons, but the outpouring of love from so many people and the knowledge of being surrounded by the Lord's care carried us through. Being parted from our daughters was as harrowing as the pain I was in, and I missed them acutely. My parents were initially advised by the ward sister that it would be too traumatic for them to see us immediately. She instead recommended waiting until we had recovered to a certain extent so that this would reassure them.

Meanwhile, at home, the Lord provided an au pair, without me needing to advertise or meet with anyone. She was already employed by another friend in my Bible Study group and 'happened' to be free for a month while my friend was travelling with her children. That first au pair 'happened' to have another friend who was later free to take her place. Our daughters remember the second au pair, Pati, with particular affection even now.

The school where we lived had a disabled chairlift in place for accessing the swimming pool. Once I was able to manage this, I could exercise with the water taking my weight. There was also a physiotherapist who visited the school site routinely, who gave me enormous pain ('no pain, no gain'!) but enabled my feet to enjoy the extraordinary mobility that I have today – which is not to forget an enormous amount of prayer from many, many people around the country. I would often be humbled months, even years, later, to meet people I'd never met but who would say: 'Oh, was it you? We've been praying for you.' I was able to relate to them the wonderful ways the Lord had answered their prayers.

If asked to recall these events to people, I always include the caveat that I realise our experience may be quite different from other people's experiences. But we were graciously aware at every stage that the Lord was totally in control and felt that, although it grieved him to allow that accident, he was right there with us. His timing and his provision were so obvious, I always felt he'd 'pulled out all the stops' to support us.

The road to recovery was a long and hard one, and has lasted years, but the knowledge that all was within God's sovereign control has always been a huge comfort. I have often felt that he heard my prayer to save David from dying for a reason: God still had work for him to do. Our lives since may not have been what we had envisaged but they have been fulfilling nonetheless.

My parents' side of the story was a huge testament to God upholding and providing for them too. They were plunged into a more than full-time emergency role of looking after two children and an au pair in our home, without us and away from everything that was familiar, for many months.

The legal case, which followed our accident, went right up to the high court in London, because of the serious nature of the case. The months of mental anguish leading up to that point were grim. Again, we were blessed with a Christian solicitor, recommended by a good friend, whose support was invaluable.

The provision of a Christian counsellor helped me through a period of depression, enabling me to face up to how my life had changed and come to terms with the restrictions and repercussions. I had to acknowledge the fact that I would not be able to return to my nursing profession or even hold down any less physically demanding employment due to the damage to my feet. I also had to accept the impact of a severe head injury on my thought processes and energy levels.

We subsequently had to leave David's job at the school and

move house and area because of our physical restraints, much of the school site being on a 1 in 4 gradient. However, God 'led [us] by a straight way to a city where [we] could settle' (Psalm 107:7). He paved the way for us with a job for David, schools for the girls, a home, a church and a new life 'post-accident'.

I hope all that I have written encourages you and leads you a step closer to knowing, believing and resting in God's sovereignty for yourself. From the Advent narrative we see that God is in control of history, in the big picture and the little details. My own experience is also an example of his intricate control over all the timings in my life. Therefore I pray:

> **May the joy of the angels,**
> **the eagerness of the shepherds,**
> **the perseverance of the wise men,**
> **the obedience of Joseph and Mary,**
> **and the peace of the Christ-child**
> **be yours this Christmas;**
> **and the blessing of God Almighty,**
> **the Father, the Son and the Holy Spirit,**
> **be among you and remain with you always.**
> **Amen.**[1]

[1] Taken from *Common Worship* by the Church of England

Song: 'A Christmas blessing' by Philip Stopford

Crown him the Lord of years,
the potentate of time,
creator of the rolling spheres,
ineffably sublime.
All hail, Redeemer, hail!
for thou hast died for me;
thy praise shall never, never fail
throughout eternity.

(Taken from 'Crown him with many crowns' by
Matthew Bridges)